Easy PCs

Shelley O'Hara

Easy PCs

Copyright © 1992 by Que® Corporation

Library of Congress Catalog No.: 92-06090

ISBN 0-88022-918-7

93 92 91   6 5 4 3 2 1

Interpretation of the printing code: the rightmost double-digit number is the year of the book's printing; the rightmost single-digit number, the number of the book's printing. For example, a printing code of 92-1 shows that the first printing of the book occurred in 1992.

Screen reproductions in this book were created using Collage Plus from Inner Media, Inc., Hollis, NH.

Publisher: Lloyd J. Short

Associate Publisher: Rick Ranucci

Project Development Manager: Thomas Bennett

Book Design: Scott Cook, Karen A. Bluestein

Production Team: Jerry Ellis, Kate Godfrey, Joe Ramon, Caroline Roop, Dennis Sheehan, Christine Young, Mary Beth Wakefield

Production Editor

Cindy Morrow

Technical Editor

Jamey Marcum

Novice Reviewer

Becky Beheler

Contents at a Glance

Easy **PCs**

Contents

Easy PCs

Contents

Contents

Easy **PCs**

Contents

Easy **PCs**

Introduction

You can do just about anything with a personal computer (or *PC*). With a PC, you can type professional-looking letters, draw a map to your house, create a letterhead, balance your checkbook, create charts, inquire about stock prices, play games, do homework, learn to type, and so on, and so on. The possibilities are endless—and may be intimidating.

You can overcome any reluctance you have with learning to use a computer by realizing that you already have the manual skills to do a task. Don't think of a computer as something entirely new or foreign. Instead, think of it as a faster, easier, and more accurate way of completing tasks you used to do manually.

For instance, you might have used a typewriter to type letters. You can do the same thing with a PC and a *word processing* program (a program for manipulating—typing, rearranging, and checking—words).

To balance a budget, you might have used a pad of lined paper and a hand-held calculator. On a PC, you can balance a budget with a *spreadsheet* program (a program for manipulating—adding, subtracting, multiplying, and so on—numbers).

To store names and addresses, you might have used a Rolodex. The computer lets you store the same information by using a *database* program (a program for manipulating—finding, sorting, and rearranging—data).

The goal is the same whether you do the task manually or let the computer automate the task. Only the method differs. To use a computer, then, you do not need to learn something entirely new. You just need to learn a new (and better) method of doing the same thing.

Why Use a Computer?

A computer has the *potential* to do the following:

- Save time
- Reduce errors
- Reduce work
- Save money

The key word here is *potential*. For the computer to do anything, you have to tell it what to do. And you have to correctly tell the computer what to do. If you tell the computer to figure your expenses for a month and leave out the entry for your house payment, the total expense is not correct. If you tell the computer to send bills to all clients with accounts 30 days past due, but forget about those with accounts 60 or more days past due, a large number of past-due clients may not receive notices. Just remember that *you* are in charge of the computer.

Here are some of the benefits computers provide:

Save time. Any task that you do over and over can be done faster and more accurately on a computer. If you type the same letter 10 times a week, you can type the letter once on the computer, save it, and then open the letter when you need to use it again.

Reduce errors. Computers can reduce errors in two ways. First, computer programs often provide features that check for errors. For instance, a word processing program has a spelling checker that can check for spelling errors. Second, the computer (when told correctly what to do) doesn't make mistakes. You may total the same column of numbers 10 times and get 10 different results. The computer will not get 10 results; it will figure the same column of numbers correctly every time.

Reduce work. The computer will not take your job away. You will not sit at your desk and watch the computer work busily all day; you will still be busy too. But the computer can relieve you of repetitive work so that you can concentrate on more important tasks. For instance, the computer will not automatically enter all your invoices. But after you have entered them *once*, the computer can total the invoices, print bills, update inventory, and so on.

Save money. Saving money is a tricky benefit because you don't just buy a computer and then let the savings pile up. A computer saves you money in intangible ways. By saving time, reducing errors, and reducing work, the computer makes you more efficient. You have time to work on other projects, which potentially will make money. You have time to concentrate on doing your job better, which potentially saves money.

What Is a Computer?

Now that you know what a computer can do for you, you need to have a basic understanding about what a computer is. You don't need to know all the ins and outs of how the motherboard (a key piece of the computer) works. After all, you don't *really* know how a washing machine works, but you know how to use it. Right? The same is true of the computer. You need to know just a few key concepts. These concepts are introduced here and then covered in more detail in the Basics part.

To do anything on a personal computer, you need the following items:

- Hardware
- Software
- Operating system

Hardware is the actual machine—keyboard, monitor, and system unit. Hardware includes the items that you can see and touch.

Software refers to the programs that you run on the hardware. *Program*, *application*, and *software* are all used interchangeably. Sometimes the terms are combined: application program, software application. These terms mean the same thing.

The *operating system* is the "middle man" between you and the hardware. The operating system, called DOS (for *disk operating system*), manages files and runs programs. You cannot do anything on a computer without DOS. With DOS itself, you can do some things (copy files, for instance). When you add programs, you can do all kinds of things (as previously described).

Because DOS is basically unfriendly and ugly, you may choose to use an *operating environment*. An operating environment is the liaison between you and DOS. The most popular operating environment is Microsoft Windows. (Keep in mind that you still need DOS.) You can find more information on DOS and Microsoft Windows in the Basics part of this book.

Why You Need This Book

Learning to use a computer is not easy. To use the computer, you must master at least the DOS basics. This means that you must memorize commands, and you must type the commands in the exact format required (called the *syntax* of the command). DOS doesn't give you any clues on how to proceed. You just see a small prompt (C:>, for instance).

But don't worry. This book is designed to make learning to use your computer *easy*. This book helps the beginning user perform basic operations. You don't have to worry that you don't know enough about computers. This book teaches you all you need to know for basic operations.

You don't have to worry that you might do something wrong and ruin a program or the computer. This book points out mistakes you might make and shows you how to avoid them. This book explains what to do when you change your mind—how to escape from a situation.

Reading this book will build your confidence. You can learn what tasks are necessary to complete a particular job. After you learn the basics, you open up a world of possibilities with your computer. That first hurdle is the highest. This book will help you pass that hurdle.

How This Book Is Organized

This book is designed with you, the beginner, in mind. The book is divided into several parts:

- Introduction
- The Basics
- Task/Review
- Reference

This Introduction explains how the book is set up and how to use the book.

The next part, The Basics, outlines general information about the hardware, operating system, and software. This part explains basic terms and concepts.

The main portion of this book, Task/Review, tells you how to perform specific tasks. The first task explains how to turn on the computer.

The Reference Guide includes a software guide that defines the different application programs you can use on the computer, a troubleshooting guide that discusses common problems, a question and answer guide that answers common questions about PCs, and a glossary that provides definitions of computer terms.

How To Use This Book

This book is set up so that you can use it several different ways:

- You can read the book from start to finish, or you can start reading at any point in the book.

- You can experiment with one exercise, many exercises, or all exercises.

- You can look up specific tasks you want to accomplish, such as starting a program.

- You can flip through the book, looking at the Before and After screens, to find specific tasks.

- You can refer to the alphabetical task listing at the beginning of the Task/Review part to find a task.

- You can read just the exercise, just the review, or both the exercise and review parts.

- You can read any part of the exercises you want. You can read all of the text to see both the steps to follow and the explanation of the steps. You can read only the text in red to see just the actions to perform. You can read just the explanation to understand what happens during a particular step.

As you read, you don't have to worry about making a mistake. All tasks have an Oops! note that explains how to get out of a situation. The book also points out errors you might make.

Task section

The Task section includes numbered steps that tell you how to accomplish certain tasks, such as copying a file. The numbered steps walk you through a specific example so that you can learn the task by doing it. Blue text below the numbered steps explains the concept in more detail.

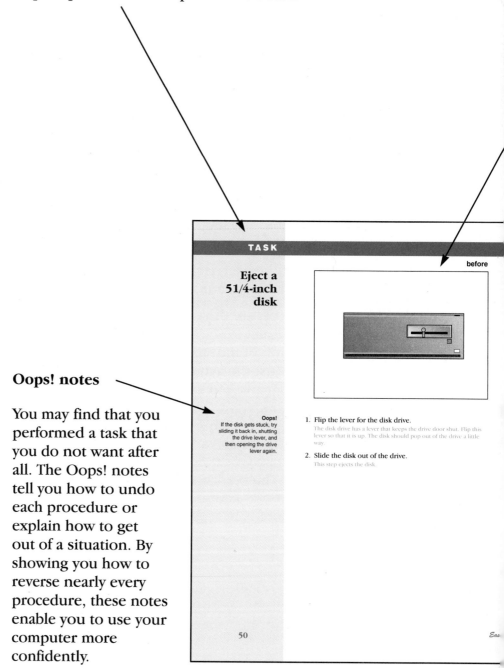

TASK

**Eject a
51/4-inch
disk**

before

Oops!
If the disk gets stuck, try
sliding it back in, shutting
the drive lever, and
then opening the drive
lever again.

1. Flip the lever for the disk drive.
   The disk drive has a lever that keeps the drive door shut. Flip this
   lever so that it is up. The disk should pop out of the drive a little
   way.

2. Slide the disk out of the drive.
   This step ejects the disk.

Oops! notes

You may find that you performed a task that you do not want after all. The Oops! notes tell you how to undo each procedure or explain how to get out of a situation. By showing you how to reverse nearly every procedure, these notes enable you to use your computer more confidently.

50

Before and After Screens

Each task includes Before and After screens that show how the computer screen will look before and after you follow the numbered steps in the Task section.

Other notes

The extra margin notes explain a little more about each procedure. These notes define terms, explain other options, and refer you to other sections, when applicable.

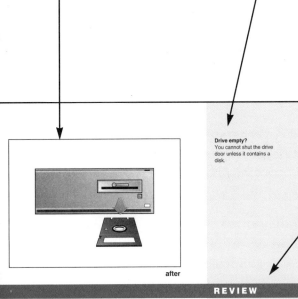

Drive empty?
You cannot shut the drive door unless it contains a disk.

after

REVIEW

1. Flip the lever for the disk drive.
2. Slide out the disk.

To eject a 5 1/4-inch disk

Use a different size disk?
If you use 3 1/2-inch disks, see *TASK: Eject a 3 1/2-inch disk.*

ng with Disks

51

Review section

After you learn a procedure by following a specific example, you can refer to the Review section for a quick summary of the task. The Review section gives you more generic steps for completing a task so that you can apply them to your own work. You can use these steps as a quick reference to refresh your memory about how to perform procedures.

How To Follow an Exercise

It would be impossible to write a book geared toward your exact equipment and programs; each computer user owns a different set of programs and a different type of computer.

Still, this book provides basic information that will help you no matter what type of computer or programs you own. This book covers many topics that pertain to all users. For instance, the information on working with disks and DOS is of interest to all users.

This book also covers some additional topics, such as Microsoft Windows. This information is useful for readers who have Microsoft Windows; they can follow along with the exercises. For those who don't have Microsoft Windows, this information is still beneficial. You can read about what you can do with Microsoft Windows to see whether you want to purchase and use this program.

The last section of this book covers some basic word processing and spreadsheet tasks. As an example, the tasks use WordPerfect for a word processing program and Excel for a spreadsheet program.

WordPerfect is the most popular word processing program; many readers may have this program. Even if you don't have this program, however, you can still learn some basic word processing skills—how to type with a word processor, how to make text bold, and so on.

Excel is used as the spreadsheet program because it is the most popular spreadsheet program for Microsoft Windows. This section—even if you don't own Excel—will teach you both how to accomplish some basic spreadsheet operations, as well as how to use a Microsoft Windows program. (Most Microsoft Windows programs are similar. You can apply what you learn in one program to other Microsoft Windows programs.)

Where To Get More Help

As you become more comfortable with a computer, you may need a more complete reference book. Que offers several books to suit your needs.

Here are some of the other Easy books published by Que:

Easy DOS

Easy Excel

Easy Lotus 1-2-3

Easy Windows, 3.1 Edition

Easy WordPerfect

Here are some additional books on DOS and Windows:

MS-DOS 5 Quick Reference

MS-DOS 5 QuickStart

Using MS-DOS 5

Windows 3.1 Quick Reference

Windows 3.1 QuickStart

Using Windows 3.1, Special Edition

Que also offers several books on specific software programs. Some of the most popular titles include the following:

Using 1-2-3 Release 2.4, Special Edition

Using Excel 4 for Windows, Special Edition

Using WordPerfect 5.1, Special Edition

Also of interest:

Introduction to Personal Computers, 2nd Edition

Que's Computer User's Dictionary, 2nd Edition

The Basics

Understanding Your Computer System

Understanding the Disk Operating System

Using an Operating Environment

Using Software

Easy **PCs**

Understanding Your Computer System

Think of your computer as just another appliance. Even though each model is different, they all have similar parts. After you use one toaster, you could probably figure out how to use any toaster. Similarly, after you start using a computer, you should be able to figure out how to use any computer.

Your computer system is made up of these basic parts:

- The system unit
- The floppy disk drive(s)
- The hard disk drive
- The monitor
- The keyboard

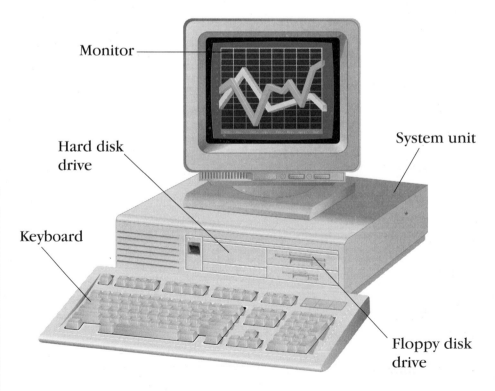

Monitor

System unit

Hard disk drive

Keyboard

Floppy disk drive

You may also have a mouse and a printer.

Easy **PCs**

System Unit. The system unit is the box that holds all the electrical components of your computer. The most important piece of the computer, the central processing unit (or CPU), is stored in the system unit. The CPU is brain of the computer. For more information, see the section *More on CPUs.* The floppy disk drive and hard disk drive are also usually inside the system unit. (The size of the system unit varies.)

Floppy Disk Drive. The floppy disk drive is the door into your computer. It allows you to put information onto the computer—onto the hard drive—and to take information off the computer—onto a floppy disk. The floppy disk drive is part of the system unit. For more information, see the section *More on Floppy Disk Drives.*

Hard Disk Drive. A hard disk drive stores the programs and files with which you work. A hard disk is usually part of the system unit. (You can attach an external disk drive that is housed in a separate case and is connected to the system unit with a cable.) See the section *More on Hard Disks.*

Monitor. The monitor displays on-screen what you type on the keyboard. Your monitor may also have a power switch. For more information, see the section *More on Monitors.*

Keyboard. You use the keyboard to communicate with the computer. You use it to type entries and to issue commands. You type on the keyboard just as you do on a regular typewriter. A keyboard also has special keys that you use. (Different computers have different keyboards.) These keys are discussed later in the section *More on Keyboards.*

Mouse. You can use the mouse, a pointing device, to move the mouse pointer on-screen, to select windows, and to issue commands. For more information, see the section *More on Mice.*

Printer. To print, you need to attach and install a printer.

More on CPUs

The CPU is the brain of the computer. This electronic component orchestrates the workings of the computer. When you press a key, the CPU interprets that key and then takes the appropriate action—for instance, it might display on-screen the character that you typed on the keyboard.

When you see advertisements for computers, the "name" of the CPU is usually mentioned. The name is really the number of the chip used in the computer. Here are the numbers used:

8086

8088

80286 (or 286 for short)

80386 (or 386 for short)

80486 (or 486 for short)

Some CPU chips are named 80386X and 80486X.

Basically, the higher the number, the newer, faster, and more expensive the chip.

The speed of the computer is determined by how fast the chip can operate. Speed is measured in megahertz, abbreviated MHz. Here are some common speeds:

12 MHz

16 MHz

25 MHz

33 MHz

Again, the higher the number, the faster (and newer) the chip. Different CPUs come in different speeds. For instance, you can have a 80386 CPU with a speed of 25 MHz or a speed of 33 MHz.

Another term you may come across as you learn about computers is RAM. RAM stands for *random-access memory* and is similar to the capacity of the CPU's brain. The more information that the CPU can remember, the faster applications can work. RAM is measured in *kilobytes* (abbreviated K) or in *megabytes* (abbreviated M). One *byte* equals about one typed character. One kilobyte equals around 1000 bytes (1024 to be exact), and one megabyte equals around 1 million bytes.

Here are some common measurements of RAM:

512K

640K

1M

4M

> **Note:** Although RAM and disk space (where you store data) are both measured in kilobytes and megabytes, they are *not* the same. RAM is a temporary storage area—much like hearing "New York, New York" playing in your head. Disk space, both floppy disk space and hard disk space, is a permanent storage area—much like a CD of *Frank Sinatra's Greatest Hits*.

More on Floppy Disk Drives

Your computer has at least one floppy disk drive. You may have more than one. The first floppy disk is named drive A, and the second drive—if you have one—is named B. The hard disk is usually named drive C.

There are two types of floppy disk drives with two matching types of disks:

- 5 1/4-inch disk drives and disks
- 3 1/2-inch disk drives and disks

Tip
If you are thinking of purchasing a computer, you should learn more about the chip, speed, and memory of the computer.

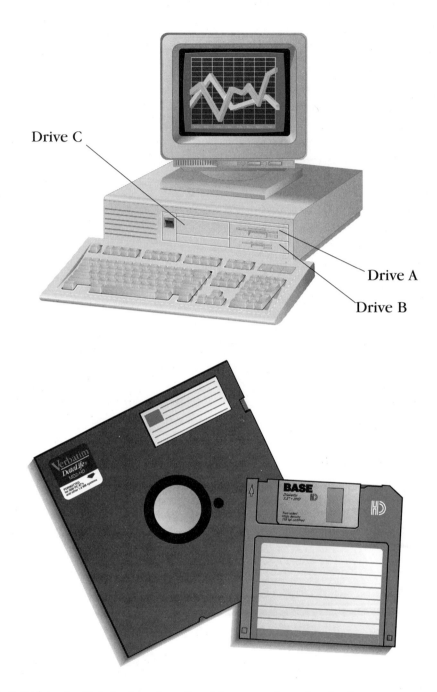

Drive C

Drive A

Drive B

A 5 1/4-inch disk is the size (in this case, the physical dimension) that the name implies—5 1/4 inches. This type of disk *is* floppy. A 3 1/2-inch disk, which is 3 1/2 inches in size, is made of hard plastic. The plastic case encloses the disk part (the floppy part).

If you have a 5 1/4-inch drive, you use 5 1/4-inch disks. If you have a 3 1/2-inch drive, you use 3 1/2-inch disks.

Floppy disks differ in size as well as in the amount of information they can store. Remember that the amount of information is measured in kilobytes (K) or in mega-bytes (M). One byte equals about one typed character. One kilobyte equals around 1000 bytes (1024 to be exact), and one megabyte equals around 1 million bytes.

5 1/4-inch disks come in two capacities: 360K and 1.2M. 360K disks are often called *double-density* or *double-sided double-density*. These disks are capable of storing around 360,000 characters of information. 1.2M disks are often called *double-sided high density*. This type of disk can store 1.2 million bytes. (Double-sided means that both types of disks store information on both sides of the disk—like a phonograph record.)

Note: The PC market is always changing. Hard disks are getting faster, and disk capacity is increasing. This book covers the most common options on the market. For instance, some manufacturers are selling "ED" drives that have a capacity of 2.88M. This book does not cover these disk types.

3 1/2-inch disks come in two capacities: 720K and 1.44M. 720K disks are often called *double-density* or *double-sided double-density* (DD). These disks are capable of storing around 720,000 characters of information. 1.44M disks are often called *double-sided high density* (HD). This type of disk can store around 1.44 million characters.

The disk drive you have must match the disk type you use. If you have a drive that can "read" only 360K disks, you should use only 360K disks. If you have a drive that can "read" 1.44M disks, you should use only 1.44M disks. (To learn what size disks your disk drive can read, you need to consult your computer manual.)

Disks are blank when you purchase them. (Some companies, however, have begun selling preformatted disks.) To prepare a disk for use, you must format it. Formatting the disk creates "cubbyholes" for data. When the operating system or a program puts something away on the disk, it keeps track of which cubbyhole it puts the data into. When the operating system or program needs that data, it goes back to that cubbyhole.

More on Hard Disks

A hard disk is similar to a floppy disk in that it stores information, but a hard disk is much larger and much faster than a floppy disk. A small hard disk may be as much as 25 times larger than a floppy disk. Hard disks are measured in *megabytes* (M or meg) or *gigabytes* (G or Gig). A gigabyte is one billion bytes. Hard disks come in various sizes: 20M, 30M, 40M, 60M, 80M, 100M, and up.

The magnetic media in a hard disk is also hard (rather than floppy) and is usually encased in the system unit. (You can add an external hard drive.) Some programs require a hard disk. This book assumes that you have a hard disk.

More on Monitors

Monitors come in different sizes, colors, and resolutions. (*Resolution* is a measure of the crispness of the image.) Here are some names of common monitor types:

CGA

EGA

VGA

Super VGA

VGA and Super VGA are the newest monitors; they have the highest resolution.

More on Keyboards

To communicate with the computer, you type commands at the keyboard. A computer keyboard is just like a typewriter, only a keyboard has additional keys:

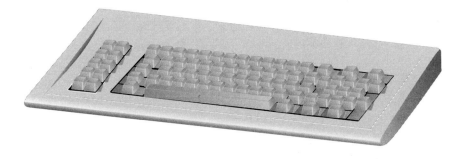

Original PC keyboard

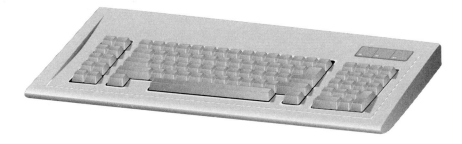

AT keyboard

Enhanced keyboard

- Arrow and other movement keys (Home, PgUp, PgDn, End)

- Function keys (F1-F10 or F1-F12)

- Text-editing keys (Backspace, Del, Ins)

- Modifier keys (Shift, Ctrl, Alt)

- Enter

- Other special keys (Print Screen, Scroll Lock, and so on)

These keys are located in different places on different keyboards. For instance, sometimes the function keys are located across the top of the keyboard. Sometimes they are on the left side of the keyboard.

You can familiarize yourself with the keyboard by reading the names of the keys. Different keys will perform different actions, depending on the program you are using. In general, the keys have the following functions:

Arrow and other movement keys. Use the arrow keys in a program to move around on-screen or to select text. Other keys, such as Home, PgUp, PgDn, and End, also move the cursor in programs. (Pressing these keys at the DOS prompt doesn't do anything.)

Function keys. Use function keys to initiate commands in programs. The command initiated depends on the program. For instance, in WordPerfect, pressing the F6 key makes text bold.

Editing keys (Backspace, Ins, Del). Use the Backspace key to delete characters. (The key is similar to a Backspace key on a typewriter, except that text is deleted when you press the Backspace key on a computer.) Del works the same way, only it deletes the character at the cursor location.

Modifier keys (Shift, Ctrl, and Alt). Use these keys to modify the action of a function key. For instance, pressing F6 in WordPerfect tells the program that you want to make text bold. Pressing and holding down Shift and then pressing F6 (Shift-F6) tells WordPerfect that you want to center text. The commands assigned to each key and key combination vary from program to program.

Shift has an additional (more traditional) use: it makes letters uppercase.

Enter. Use this key to confirm a command or, when you are typing, to insert a carriage return.

More on Mice

A mouse works with a keyboard and is another type of input device. (You still need a keyboard because you cannot type with the mouse.) Certain actions, such as drawing, are easier with the mouse. Some programs let you use a mouse, some don't.

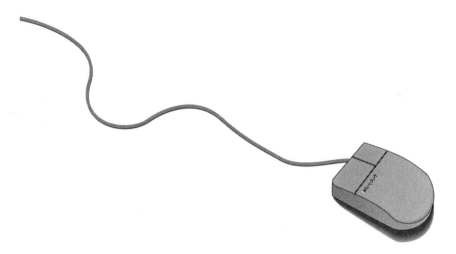

You use the mouse by sliding it on the desktop. The mouse pointer moves on-screen. Here are some of the things you can do with a mouse:

- Select text
- Select menu commands
- Move the insertion point
- Draw graphic objects

There are four types of mouse actions:

Term	Action
Point	Place the mouse pointer on an item. Be sure to place the *tip* of the mouse pointer on the item.
Click	Point to an item, press the left mouse button, and release the mouse button.
Double-click	Point to an item and press the left mouse button twice in rapid succession.
Drag	Point to an item. Press and hold down the left mouse button, and then move the mouse. After the item you are dragging is where you want it, release the mouse button.

Keep these terms in mind as you follow some of the tasks in this book.

Understanding the Disk Operating System

Now that you are familiar with the physical parts of the machine, you need to have a little understanding of what goes on behind the scenes.

When you first turn on the computer, DOS is loaded or started. Loading the operating system is called "booting" the computer. DOS is the operating system—the "middle man" between you and the hardware. To use your computer, you must have DOS.

On-screen you see a blank screen with a small prompt. This prompt is called the *DOS prompt*. The following screen shows a DOS prompt:

From this prompt, you issue commands to start programs, copy files, and perform other tasks. The DOS section of this book covers some specific DOS tasks. The following sections describe DOS and its file management system.

Directories and Files

Think about how you store items in your office—you may have a filing cabinet. In that filing cabinet, you probably have folders that pertain to different projects (or clients or patients or some other grouping—maybe logical, maybe not). Within each folder you have articles, letters, diagrams, reports—anything you want to save. This storage method carries over to DOS.

With DOS, a disk is like a filing cabinet. Within that disk, you have *directories*—areas set aside for certain files (memos, articles, diagrams). The same items that you store in a folder are stored in electronic form in a file, and that file is stored in a directory.

Filing cabinet (Disk)

Individual documents
(Files)

Folders (Directories)

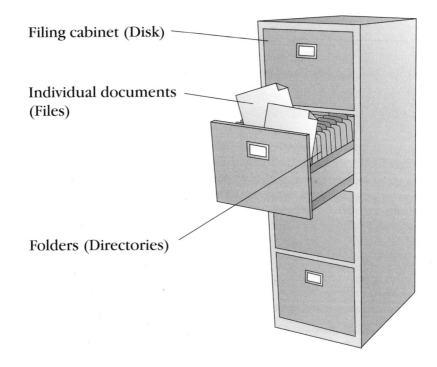

Root Directory and the Path

The main directory is called the *root directory*. All other directories are branches of this directory. (Picture the roots of a tree.) Directories can contain files, programs, or other directories.

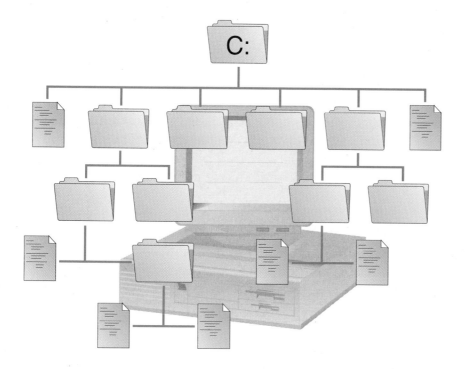

To get to a particular file, you must trace the path from the root directory to the directory that contains the file. The *path* is the list of directories, starting with the root. Each directory name is separated by a backslash. For instance, the path

```
C:\WORD\REPORTS
```

gives you these directions: Start at drive C, go from the root directory (\), to WORD, then to REPORTS, as the following diagram illustrates:

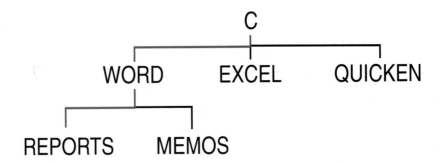

File Names

Each file must have a unique or different name. A file's name is made up of the file name (up to eight characters) and an optional extension (up to three characters). The file name and extension are separated by a period. You cannot use the following characters in a file name:

' " / \ [ ] : ;

REPORT.DOC is a valid file name. REPORT is the file name, and DOC is the extension. The file name should tell you what the report contains; the extension often tells you the type of file. Some programs assign an extension automatically.

MY NOTES is not a valid file name. You cannot include spaces in a file name.

EASYDOSBOOK.DOC is not a valid file name because it contains too many characters.

Extensions usually identify file types. Here is a list of common extensions and their meaning:

BAK	backup file
BAT	batch file
COM	program file
DOC	document file
EXE	program (executable) file
WKS	worksheet file

Special Files

Your computer contains some files that perform special functions:

To process commands, you must have a file called COMMAND.COM. This is a special DOS file that displays the DOS prompt and executes commands. When you install DOS on a disk, this file is copied.

When you start DOS, it looks for a file called AUTOEXEC.BAT. You may or may not have this file. If you do have the file, it must be stored in the root directory. When DOS starts and finds the file, the file is executed. This file may include commands that control different settings. For instance, it might include a command that tells DOS where your programs are located. This command is called a *path* command.

The following shows a simple AUTOEXEC.BAT file:

```
PROMPT $P$G

PATH C:\DOS;C:\WP51
```

This file changes your prompt (C:\) so that it displays the current subdirectory. For instance, if you are in the directory DATA, which is a subdirectory of C:\WP51, you would see

```
C:\WP51\DATA>
```

The PATH command tells DOS to look in the directories DOS and WP51 for program files.

Another special file that DOS uses when it starts up is CONFIG.SYS, a configuration file. Some applications require special commands. These commands are contained in the CONFIG.SYS file. You may or may not have this file.

The following shows a simple CONFIG.SYS file:

```
FILES=20

BUFFERS=25
```

These settings control how DOS uses files; some programs require that these are set to a certain value.

When dealing with these files, keep in mind the following rules:

- Don't delete any of these files: COMMAND.COM, AUTOEXEC.BAT, or CONFIG.SYS.

- Don't try to edit COMMAND.COM.

- As you add applications to the computer, the program manual may tell you to make changes to the AUTOEXEC.BAT file or the CONFIG.SYS file. You must use a special text editor to modify these files. Be careful when making any changes. You should understand each command in the file before changing anything.

DOS Versions

You may have heard DOS called MS-DOS or PC DOS. For all practical purposes, they are the same. DOS is DOS.

DOS is updated periodically: new commands are added, other commands are made to work better, bugs (problems) are fixed. The most current DOS version is 5.0.

The Shell

Provided with DOS 5.0 is a shell. (DOS 4.0 also had a shell, but it worked differently than it does in the new version.)

The *shell* is a program that acts as a user interface to DOS. Rather than use the command line to enter commands, you can enter commands through the shell. The DOS Shell looks like this:

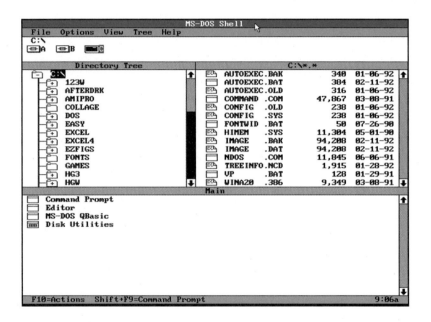

This book does not cover how to use the DOS Shell. For more information, see Que's *Easy DOS*.

Using an Operating Environment

If you are intimidated by DOS, you might want to use an operating environment. An *operating environment* is like a layer over DOS. (Everything you just read about DOS still applies to an operating environment.) An operating environment is often described as a GUI (pronounced "gooey"). This acronym stands for *graphical user interface*. The most common GUI is Microsoft Windows. The Microsoft Windows screen looks like this:

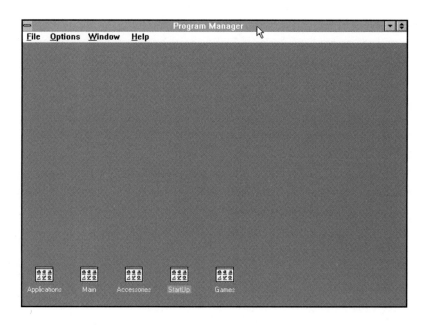

Keep the following in mind: The bare bones operating system is DOS. DOS with some frills is the DOS Shell. DOS all dolled up is Microsoft Windows. You can have one, two, or all three, but you still must have DOS.

Microsoft Windows uses a desktop metaphor. Rather than displaying a blank screen when you start, Microsoft Windows displays a desktop with windows and icons. (*Icons* are pictures that represent other windows or programs.) This visual approach allows you to point to what you want by using the mouse. Starting a program, for example, is simply a matter of pointing at the program that you want and clicking the mouse.

The Benefits of Microsoft Windows

With Microsoft Windows you can do the following:

Start programs. Rather than memorize and type commands to start a program, you point to the program you want and click the mouse. The program opens on-screen in a window.

Manage files.   You can use Microsoft Windows to display files, copy files, move files, rename files, and perform other file-management tasks. You can select commands from a menu (rather than type them). And you can display files in a window on-screen. You can display several windows at once.

Use Microsoft Windows desk accessories.   Included with Microsoft Windows are a color paint program, a word processor, a calendar, a calculator, a notepad, a cardfile, two games, and other programs. You can use these programs to draw logos, create documents, schedule appointments, solve equations, type notes, store addresses, and have fun.

Display more than one window at a time.   When you work on a project, you don't just have one sheet of paper on your desk; you have several. One sheet might contain sales projections; one might be your current inventory list; one might be notes from sales representatives. Using all of these pieces of information, you can create a report. Working with Microsoft Windows is the same way. You can display the information you need in several windows and then move among the windows.

Run two programs at once.   If you have enough memory, you can run two programs at once and switch between them. You can enter figures in a worksheet and then pull those figures into a word-processing document.

Use Microsoft Windows programs.   Many programs are designed specifically to work with Microsoft Windows. These programs work essentially in the same way. After you learn one Microsoft Windows program, you can easily learn other Microsoft Windows programs, and experiment with those you haven't yet learned.

The Microsoft Windows Desktop

After you start Microsoft Windows, you see the desktop. (If you want to start the program and follow along, see *TASK: Start Microsoft Windows* in the Microsoft Windows section.)

To use Microsoft Windows effectively, you should learn the different parts of the screen:

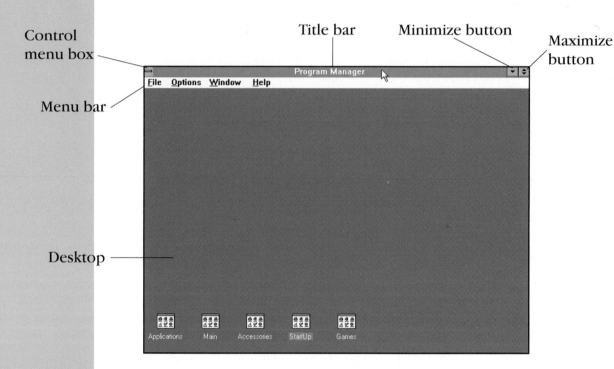

The desktop is the screen background that displays the windows and icons.

The title bar displays the name of the window.

The Control menu box lets you manipulate windows. Click on this menu box to display a menu. Double-click on this menu box to close a window.

The Maximize and Minimize buttons are used to size windows. See *TASK: Maximize a window* and *TASK: Minimize a window* later in the Microsoft Windows section of the Task/Review part.

The menu bar is used to select commands.

This book includes a section on some basic Microsoft Windows skills, and the section on spreadsheets covers a Microsoft Windows program (Excel).

Using Software

You need hardware and an operating system; these components are essentially a PC. But you cannot accomplish much practical work with just the hardware and DOS or with just the hardware and DOS and Microsoft Windows. To make the PC work, you need software. *Software* refers to the programs you use. *Software*, *application*, and *program* all mean the same thing.

Think of a program as a specialist hired to perform a task. For instance, you might need an accountant to do your budget and taxes, a typist to do mailings, an artist to create a logo, a stockbroker to quote stock prices, and so on. Rather than hire a specialist, you use a program. For accounting tasks, you might use a spreadsheet program. For typing letters, you would use a word processor. To create maps and letters, you would employ a drawing program. Each of these programs runs on the PC.

There are many different types of software programs; the Software Guide in the Reference part explains the different types of software along with their benefits. In this section, you will consider how to select software.

Choosing a Software Program

To make your work productive, you must select your software carefully. Here are some guidelines:

- Make a list of what you want the computer to do. Do you want to type letters? Create a budget? Generate mailing lists? Do all three? Have a definite goal in mind.

- Think about how you do the task manually. Collect any papers or forms that you currently use. Use these materials to help define the list of tasks you want to accomplish on a computer.

- Think about what you want the computer to do three years from now. You will be amazed at how quickly you learn tasks on a computer. Today you might just want to type a simple letter. Next month you might be creating your own newsletter.

- Think about how much money you want to spend. Full-featured programs will be more expensive than programs with fewer features.

- Do a little research. Pick up a computer magazine and read the ads and reviews.

Verifying That You Can Run a Software Program

After you decide what software you want, you need to make sure that you can run it on your computer. Most software packages list the hardware and operating system requirements somewhere on the outside of the software package.

This requirement list will usually tell you the following:

- The type of computer you need (80386, for example)

- The amount of RAM (640K, for example)

- The amount of hard disk space (480K, for example)

- The DOS version (3.0 or higher, for example)

The list may also tell you the types of printers and monitors you can use, as well as other information.

Be sure that your computer is capable of running the program. If you don't know what type of computer you have, the amount of RAM, hard disk space, or DOS version, check with your dealer.

Task/Review

Working with Disks

Working with DOS

Working with Microsoft Windows

Using a Word Processing Program (WordPerfect)

Using a Spreadsheet Program (Excel)

Easy **PCs**

Easy **PCs**

Working with Disks

This section includes the following tasks:

Turn on the computer

Turn off the computer

Turn on the printer

Insert a 5 1/4-inch disk

Eject a 5 1/4-inch disk

Write-protect a 5 1/4-inch disk

Insert a 3 1/2-inch disk

Eject a 3 1/2-inch disk

Write-protect a 3 1/2-inch disk

Turn on the computer

before

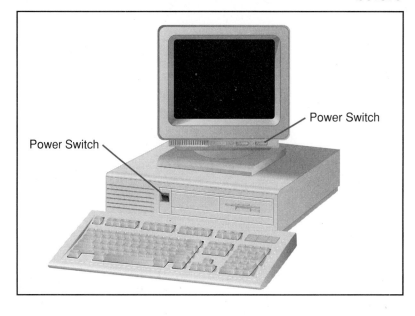

Power Switch

Power Switch

Oops!
If you don't see the DOS prompt, be sure that you turned on both the computer and monitor. If you have plugged the computer and monitor into a powerstrip, be sure that the strip is plugged in and turned on.

1. **Turn on the computer and monitor.**

   Every computer has a different location for its power switch. Check the side, the front, and the back of your computer. You also may need to turn on your monitor; it may have a separate power switch.

   DOS starts automatically when you turn on your computer. You may see information on-screen as DOS goes through its startup routine. For more information on DOS, see the next section, Working with DOS.

   On some computers, you simply have to turn on the computer and can skip the following two steps. Other computers, however, prompt you for the date and time. If your computer prompts you for the date and time, follow steps 2 and 3.

2. **If you are prompted, type the current date and press Enter.**

   When you first turn on the computer, some systems ask you to enter the current date. (Many of the newer models enter the time and date automatically. If you aren't prompted for these entries, don't worry.)

3. **If you are prompted, type the current time and press Enter.**

   If you are prompted for the date, you will also be prompted for the time.

after

You see the DOS prompt on-screen (usually C:\>). The DOS prompt may appear differently on your computer. (You can change the prompt if you want. See *Easy DOS* or *Using MS-DOS 5* for more information. This book displays the directory name as part of the prompt.)

1. Turn on the computer and monitor.

2. If you are prompted, type the current date and press **Enter**.

3. If you are prompted, type the current time and press **Enter**.

To turn on the computer

Turn off the computer

Oops!
To turn on the computer,
see *TASK: Turn on the computer.*

before

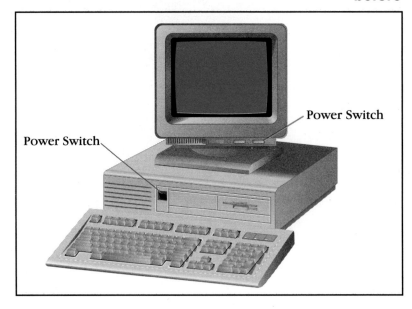

Power Switch

Power Switch

1. **Exit all programs.**

   You should turn off the computer only when you are at a DOS prompt. If you are working in a program, save all files and exit the program before you turn off the computer. (See your application manual for help with saving and exiting.)

2. **Turn off the computer and the monitor (if necessary).**

   Every computer has a different location for its power switch. Check the side, the front, and the back of your computer. You also may need to turn off your monitor; it may have a separate power switch.

   Some people say you should leave the computer on most of the time—even when you are not using it. Others say you should turn it off each time you finish using it. You can turn your computer off or leave it on when you finish using it—whatever makes you most comfortable.

after

1. Exit all programs so that you return to the DOS prompt.

2. Turn off the computer and monitor.

To turn off computer

Turn on the printer

before

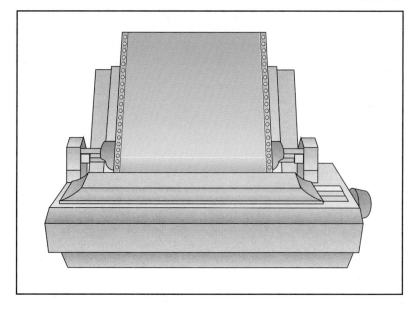

Press the power switch.

Every printer has a different location for its power switch. Check the side, the front, and the back of your printer. When you turn on the printer, the lights on the control panel are lit.

Turning on the printer automatically puts the printer on-line (ready for use). You can take it off line—for instance, to eject a piece of paper—by pressing the on-line button. You will find the on-line button on the printer's control panel. The name of the button varies between different printers; the button name may be Select, On-Line, or something similar.

Depending on the the type of printer you use, it may go through a startup routine and may print a test page.

Easy **PCs**

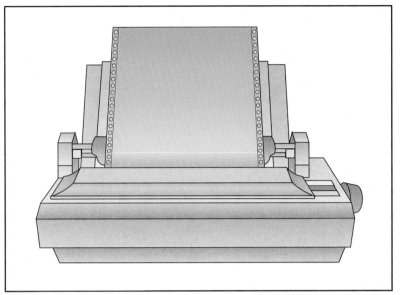

after

A note on different printers
Different printers have different control panels. The control panel is similar to the computer's keyboard. You communicate to the printer by pressing the appropriate button or combination of buttons.

Press the power switch.

To turn on the printer

For more information
For more information on the use of your printer, see your printer manual.

Insert a 5 1/4-inch disk

before

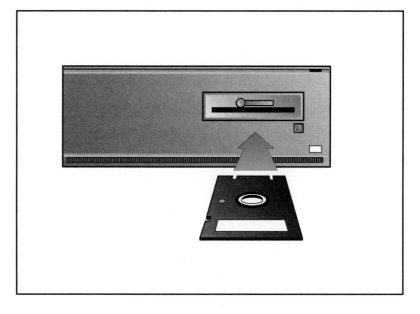

Oops!
You cannot shut the lever if a disk is not inserted properly into the drive. If the lever will not shut, take out the disk and try inserting it again.

1. **Hold the disk so that the label is facing up.**

   Just as you shouldn't insert a VCR tape upside down, you also shouldn't insert a floppy disk upside down.

   Hold the disk so that the notched side is on the left. (Disk types are described in the Basics part.)

2. **Insert the disk into the drive.**

   Push the disk gently—don't force it into the drive.

3. **Shut the drive door.**

   The drive door has a lever or latch. Push down the lever. For the computer to be able to look at (read) and store (write) information on the disk, the lever must be shut.

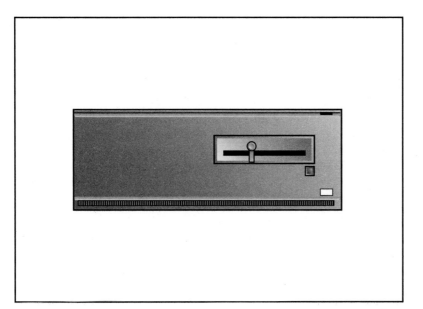

after

Be careful!
Never force the door shut.
If the disk doesn't slide in
easily, be sure that you
are inserting it properly.

1. Hold the disk label up.

2. Insert the disk into the drive.

3. Shut the drive door.

To insert a 5 1/4-inch disk

Use a different size disk?
If you use 3 1/2-inch
disks, see *TASK: Insert
a 3 1/2-inch disk.*

Eject a 51/4-inch disk

before

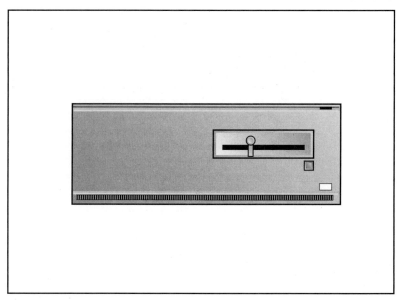

Oops!
If the disk gets stuck, try sliding it back in, shutting the drive lever, and then opening the drive lever again.

1. **Flip the lever for the disk drive.**

   The disk drive has a lever that keeps the drive door shut. Flip this lever so that it is up. The disk should pop out of the drive a little way.

2. **Slide the disk out of the drive.**

   This step ejects the disk.

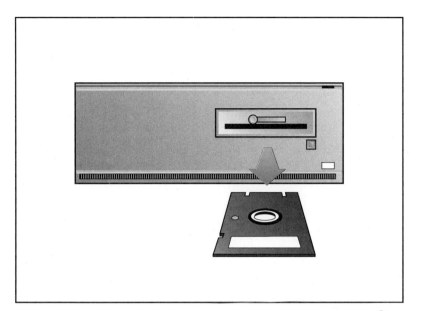

after

Drive empty?
You cannot shut the drive door unless it contains a disk.

1. Flip the lever for the disk drive.

2. Slide out the disk.

To eject a 5 1/4-inch disk

Use a different size disk?
If you use 3 1/2-inch disks, see *TASK: Eject a 3 1/2-inch disk.*

Write-protect a 5 1/4-inch disk

before

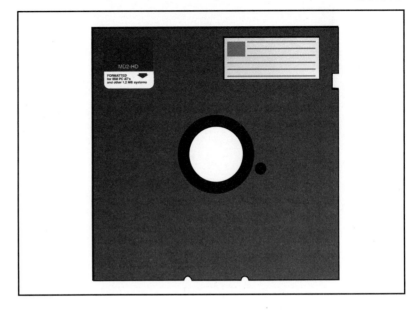

Oops!
To remove the write-protection, pull off the tab.

1. **Find the write-protect tabs that came with the disks.**

   When you purchased your disks, you should have received disk labels and write-protect tabs. The tabs are probably silver or black, and they are adhesive—like tape.

2. **Cover the write-protect notch with the tab.**

   This step write-protects the disk. You (or anyone else) cannot delete or change any of the files on the disk when it is write-protected. (You can still copy and open files; you just cannot delete or change them.)

   To cover the notch, wrap the tab over the notch so that half of the tab covers the notch on one side and half of the tab covers the notch on the other side.

Easy **PCs**

Write-
protect
tab

after

Cover the write-protect notch with a write-protect tab.

Don't have any tabs?
If you don't have any write-protect tabs, you can use transparent tape.

To write-protect a 5 1/4-inch disk

Write-protect program disks
When you are installing a new program, be sure to write-protect the program disks. That way, you will not write over the information.

Working with Disks

53

Insert a 3 1/2-inch disk

before

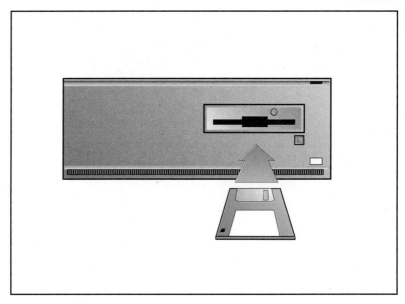

1. **Hold the disk so that the label is facing up.**

   Just as you shouldn't insert a VCR tape upside down, you also shouldn't insert a floppy disk upside down.

   If the disk does not have a label, it will still probably have some kind of writing (such as the disk type, an arrow, or the name of the manufacturer) on the "up" side. Hold the disk so that you see the writing.

2. **Insert the disk into the drive.**

   Push the disk gently—don't force it into the drive. You should hear a click, which indicates that the disk is inserted.

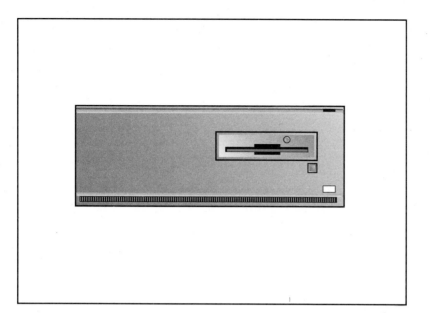

after

Be careful!
Never force a disk into the disk drive. If it doesn't slide in easily, check to be sure that you are inserting it properly.

1. Hold the disk label up.

2. Insert the disk into the drive.

To insert a 3 1/2-inch disk

Use a different size disk?
If you use 5 1/4-inch disks, see *TASK: Insert a 5 1/4-inch disk.*

Eject a 3 1/2-inch disk

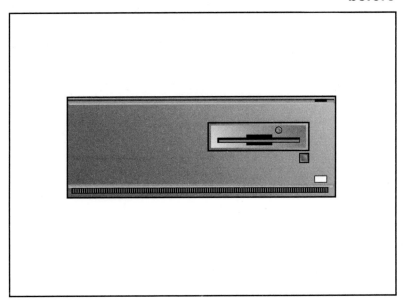

Oops!
If the disk gets stuck, try sliding it back in, and then push the button again.

1. **Push the drive door button.**

   The disk drive has a button that keeps the drive door shut. When the drive contains a disk, this button pops out. Pushing on the button ejects the disk.

2. **Slide the disk out of the drive.**

   This step takes the disk out of the drive.

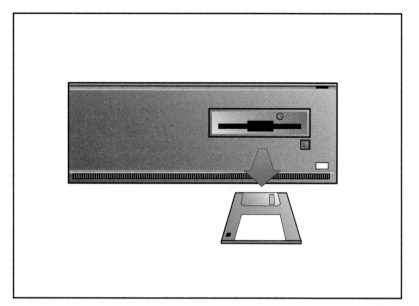

after

Can't push the button?
If you cannot push the button because it is already pushed in, the disk drive does not contain a disk.

1. Push the drive button.
2. Slide out the disk.

To eject a 3 1/2-inch disk

Use a different size disk?
If you use 5 1/4-inch disks, see *TASK: Eject a 5 1/4-inch disk.*

Write-protect a 3 1/2-inch disk

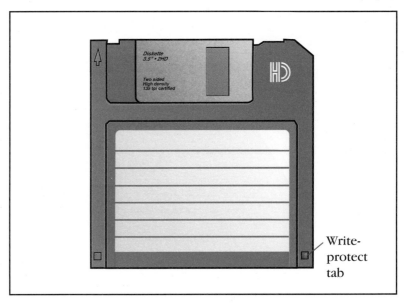

Write-protect tab

Oops!
To unprotect the disk, slide the tab so that you cannot see a small square hole.

1. **Turn over the disk.**

   This step shows you the back of the disk. You should see a metal hub in the center of the disk. In the lower right corner is a black slider tab.

2. **Slide the tab down so that you can see through a small square hole on the disk.**

   This step write-protects the disk. You (or anyone else) cannot delete any of the files on the disk when it is write-protected. (You can still copy and open files; you just can't delete or change them.)

   If you cannot slide the tab with your fingers, use a pen to push the tab.

Easy **PCs**

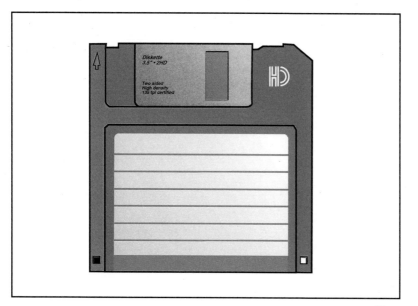

after

See another hole?
Some disks have two square holes. The second square does not have a black tab and is on the other side of the disk. Don't worry about this hole; it simply indicates the disk type.

To write-protect a 3 1/2-inch disk

Write-protect program disks
When you are installing a new program, be sure to write-protect the program disks. That way, you will not write over the information.

1. Turn over the disk.

2. Slide the write-protect tab down so that you can see through a small square hole on the disk.

Working with DOS

This section includes the following tasks:

Start DOS

Restart DOS

Type a DOS command

See what is on a disk

Clear the screen

Make a directory

Change to a different directory

Change to the root directory

Change to a different drive

Copy a file

Copy a file to another directory

Rename a file

Delete a file

Delete all files

Remove a directory

Start a DOS program

Exit a DOS program

Start DOS

before

Oops!
If you don't see the DOS prompt, be sure that you turned on both the computer and monitor. If the computer and monitor are plugged into a powerstrip, be sure that the strip is plugged in and turned on.

1. Turn on the computer and monitor.

Every computer has a different location for its power switch. Check the side, the front, and the back of your computer. You also may need to turn on your monitor; it may have a separate power switch.

You may see information on-screen as the computer goes through its startup routine. Some systems check the memory. You may see something like 256 OK, 512 OK, and so on. You may see different commands on-screen. These commands tell you that DOS is checking several areas to make sure that it will run correctly. Then DOS is loaded.

Remember that DOS starts and then looks for the CONFIG.SYS file. If DOS finds this file, it executes the commands in that file. DOS then looks for the AUTOEXEC.BAT file. If it finds this file, it executes the commands in that file. (These files are discussed in the Basics part.)

On some computers, you simply have to turn on the computer and can skip the following two steps. Other computers, however, prompt you for the date and time. If your computer prompts you for a date, follow steps 2 and 3.

2. If you are prompted, type the current date and press Enter.

When you first turn on the computer, some systems ask you to enter the current date. (Many of the newer models enter the time and date automatically. If you aren't prompted for these entries, don't worry.)

Easy **PCs**

`C:\>`

after

3. If you are prompted, type the current time and press **Enter**.

If you are prompted for the date, you will also be prompted for the time.

You see the DOS prompt on-screen (usually `C:\>`). The DOS prompt may appear differently on your computer. (You can change the prompt if you want. See *Easy DOS* or *Using MS-DOS 5* for more information. This book displays the directory name as part of the prompt.)

1. Turn on the computer and monitor.

2. If you are prompted, type the current date and press **Enter**.

3. If you are prompted, type the current time and press **Enter**.

To start DOS

Enter the correct date and time
Your computer uses the date and time to keep track of when you save files to disk. Therefore, be sure to enter the correct date and time so that your file information is accurate.

Restart DOS

before

1. **Press and hold down Ctrl, Alt, and Del.**

   You must press all three keys at once. That is, press and hold down the Ctrl key. Keeping Ctrl held down, press and hold down the Alt key. Then, keeping Ctrl and Alt held down, press the Del key. (Pressing several keys at once is called a "key combination," and is often indicated with hyphens; for example: Ctrl-Alt-Del.)

   Pressing these three keys together tells DOS to start over.

   Often you will restart if a program freezes up (stops working) when you are completing a task. Notice that in the Before screen, a spreadsheet program froze.

2. **Release all three keys.**

   This process is called a *warm boot* or a *soft boot*. DOS will run through its startup routine and execute the CONFIG.SYS and AUTOEXEC.BAT files. In a warm boot, DOS skips some of the checks it performs during a cold boot. (A *cold boot* is when you turn off the machine and then turn it on again.) A cold boot is harder on your hardware. Always try a warm boot first.

Easy **PCs**

C:\>

after

Why restart?
If the system "hangs" (doesn't respond to your commands), you may need to restart. Also, if you change a key file (AUTOEXEC.BAT or CONFIG.SYS), you must reboot to make the changes take effect.

REVIEW

Press **Ctrl-Alt-Del**.

To restart DOS

Be careful!
Using the Ctrl-Alt-Del key combination is an escape from some situations, but you should reboot only when nothing else works or when a program tells you to do so.

Type a DOS command

before

Oops!
Before you press Enter, you can correct any typing mistakes by pressing the Backspace key. Pressing the Backspace key deletes the character to the left of the cursor.

1. **From the DOS prompt, type DIR.**

   DIR is the directory command. This command shows you the contents of the current directory.

   Each DOS command has a special name and format called the "syntax." The format may include switches—options you add to the end of the command to control how the command works.

2. **Press Enter.**

   Pressing Enter confirms the command. You can make changes to the command before you press Enter.

Easy **PCs**

```
C:\>DIR
```

after

Bad command?
If you see the message Bad command or file name, you typed the command incorrectly. Try again.

1. Type the command.

2. Press **Enter**.

To type a DOS command

Upper- or lowercase?
You can type the command in either upper- or lowercase letters. The case does not matter. DOS considers DIR, dir, and Dir to be the same command.

See what is on a disk

Oops!
If you see the message
Bad command or file
name, you typed the
command incorrectly.
Try again.

before

```
C:\>DIR
```

1. **From the DOS prompt, type DIR.**

   DIR is the directory command. It tells DOS to list all of the files in the current directory. In this example, the current directory is the root (or main directory). See *TASK: Change to a different directory* for information on changing the directory.

2. **Press Enter.**

   Pressing Enter confirms the command. You see a list of the files and directories in the root directory. (Your list will vary from the list in the After screen, depending on the files and directories that your disk contains.)

   Note that the following information appears on-screen:

File name	The first part of the file name (up to eight characters long) appears first.
Extension	The extension (up to three characters long) is listed in the second column.
File Size	The next column lists the size of the file. The size is measured in *bytes*. One byte equals around one character. If the entry is a directory, nothing is listed.
Directory	If the entry is a directory, you see <DIR> in the next column.
Date	The next column displays the date that the file was created or modified.
Time	The final column displays the time that the file was created or modified.

Easy **PCs**

```
C:\>DIR

 Volume in drive C has no label
 Volume Serial Number is 16A9-592C
 Directory of C:\

AMIPRO       <DIR>     12-13-91    3:29p
123R23       <DIR>     01-29-90    9:51a
123R3        <DIR>     01-29-90    9:51a
CONFIG   SYS      441  01-07-92    2:47p
WPWIN        <DIR>     08-23-91   12:46a
WS4          <DIR>     11-04-91    8:56p
WPC          <DIR>     08-23-91   12:47a
AUTOEXEC BAT      612  01-07-92    3:17p
QA           <DIR>     02-06-90   12:05p
DBASE        <DIR>     02-13-90   11:56a
COMMAND  COM    47845  04-09-91    5:00a
PROCOM       <DIR>     11-18-91    2:53a
        12 file(s)       48898 bytes
                       1337344 bytes free

C:\>
```

after

The two lines at the end of the directory listing display the number of files, bytes taken, and bytes free (disk space remaining).

The DOS prompt is displayed at the bottom of the listing so that you can type another command.

1. From the DOS prompt, type **DIR**.

2. Press **Enter**.

To see what is on a disk

Files scroll off the screen?
If files scroll off the screen so that you cannot see the entire list, you have too many files to display on one screen. In this case, display a wide listing or pause the display. (Type DIR /W or DIR /P. See *Easy DOS* for more information.)

Change drives
To see the files on another drive, such as a floppy drive, change to that drive and then type DIR. See *TASK: Change to a different drive.*

Clear the screen

before

```
C:\>DIR

  Volume in drive C is SEO'S DISK
  Directory of  C:\

HARDCARD    <DIR>        9-04-91   12:10a
DOS         <DIR>        5-18-91   12:16a
CONFIG   SYS      10   10-23-90    1:02a
AUTOEXEC OLD      98    9-04-91   12:49a
DATA        <DIR>        9-04-91   12:39a
COMMAND  COM   25307    3-17-87   12:00p
AUTOEXEC BAT     128    8-28-91   12:02a
TREEINFO NCD     299    9-04-91   12:18a
FRECOVER DAT   38912   10-12-91   12:00a
FRECOVER BAK   38912   10-12-91   12:00a
COLLAGE     <DIR>        8-28-91   12:01a
WORD5       <DIR>        5-18-91   12:03a
NU          <DIR>        5-18-91   12:17a
CHOICE      <DIR>        5-18-91   12:20a
WP51        <DIR>        5-18-91   12:23a
QPRO        <DIR>        6-24-91    2:46a
       16 File(s)   4431872 bytes free

C:\>CLS
```

Oops!
If you see the message
Bad command or file
name, you typed the
command incorrectly.
Try again.

1. **At the DOS prompt, type CLS.**

   The CLS command tells DOS to clear the screen.

2. **Press Enter.**

   Pressing Enter confirms the command. The current screen
   information is cleared so that all you see is the DOS prompt at the
   top of the screen.

Easy **PCs**

C:\>

after

1. At the DOS prompt, type **CLS**.

2. Press **Enter**.

To clear the screen

Make a directory

before

```
C:\>MD \DATA
```

Oops!
If you see the message
`Directory already
exists`, a directory already
exists that has
the same name as the
directory you are trying
to create. Simply rename
the new directory.

1. **At the DOS prompt, type MD.**

   MD is the make directory command. This command tells DOS to create a directory.

2. **Type \DATA.**

   DATA is the name of the directory that you want to create. The backslash (\) tells DOS to make this a directory of the root directory. (The backslash represents the root directory.)

3. **Press Enter.**

   Pressing Enter confirms the command, and DOS creates the directory. The entire command is MD\DATA. Keep in mind that the directory you started from is still the current directory; you have only created a directory, you have not made that new directory the current directory. (To change directories, see *TASK: Change to a different directory*.)

   Also, note that you cannot rename a directory after you create it, so be sure to type the name correctly when you create the directory.

   You return to the DOS prompt.

4. **Type DIR and press Enter.**

   This step displays the directory listing on-screen so that you can see the new directory entry.

```
Volume in drive C is HARD DISK
Volume Serial Number is 1724-0637
Directory of C:\

HARDCARD      <DIR>        09-04-91  12:10a
DOS           <DIR>        05-18-91  12:16a
CONFIG   SYS         74    09-04-91  12:49a
DATA          <DIR>        09-04-91  12:24a
OLD_DOS  1    <DIR>        09-04-91  12:39a
WINA20   386       9349    04-09-91   5:00a
AUTOEXEC BAT         98    09-04-91  12:49a
TREEINFO NCD        299    09-04-91  12:18a
FRECOVER DAT      38912    09-04-91  12:00a
FRECOVER BAK      38912    09-04-91  12:00a
COLLAGE       <DIR>        08-28-91  12:01a
WORD5         <DIR>        05-18-91  12:03a
NU            <DIR>        05-18-91  12:17a
CHOICE        <DIR>        05-18-91  12:20a
WP51          <DIR>        05-18-91  12:23a
COMMAND  COM      47845    04-09-91   5:00a
QPRO          <DIR>        06-24-91   2:46a
       17 file(s)      135489 bytes
                      2711552 bytes free

C:\>
```

after

1. At the DOS prompt, type MD.

2. Type the complete name of the directory (including the backslash and the path).

3. Press Enter.

To make a directory

Why make a directory?
Directories are similar to file folders; they enable you to organize your files. Rather than have files scattered everywhere, you can organize them by type or application. For instance, you may create a directory that will contain all your memos.

What is a path?
A path is the route to a file. Starting from the disk drive, it tells DOS where to store or find the file.

Change to a different directory

```
C:\>CD\DATA
```

1. **At the DOS prompt, type CD.**

   CD is the change directory command. It tells DOS to change to a different directory.

2. **Type \DATA.**

   \DATA is the directory name. (If you don't have this directory, type one that you do have.)

3. **Press Enter.**

   Pressing Enter confirms the command. The entire command is CD\DATA.

   If your prompt displays the current directory, you see C:\DATA>. This prompt reminds you that you are in the DATA directory. (Your prompt may still display just C:\>. See *Easy DOS* or *Using MS-DOS 5* for information about changing your prompt.)

   Remember that the path tells DOS where to find the directory, so you must type the entire path or route to the command. If the directory is part of another directory, you must type the entire name. For instance, if DATA is contained in the directory WORD and you are starting from the root directory, you must type CD\WORD\DATA. You cannot type CD\DATA (and skip WORD).

```
C:\>CD\DATA
C:\DATA>
```

after

1. At the DOS prompt, type **CD**.

2. Type the directory name. Be sure to type the entire path.

3. Press **Enter**.

To change to a different directory

Why change directories?
After you are in the new directory, you can display a directory listing, start a program, copy files, and so on. CD is an important command; it enables you to navigate around the directory structure—move from directory to directory.

Try this tip
To back up one directory (move to the directory that contains the current directory), type CD.. (two periods). This command tells DOS to move back one directory. If you are at the C:\WP\DATA> prompt, for example, you can type CD.. to go to the C:\WP> prompt (directory).

Change to the root directory

1. **At the DOS prompt, type CD.**

   CD is the change directory command. This command tells DOS to make a different directory active.

2. **Type \.**

   The backslash (\) is the name for the root directory. Typing this character tells DOS that you want to return to the root directory.

3. **Press Enter.**

   Pressing Enter confirms the command. You return to the root directory.

```
C:\DATA>CD\

C:\>
```

after

Return from anywhere
The CD\ command enables you to return to the root directory from any other directory.

To change to the root directory

1. At the DOS prompt, type **CD**.

2. Press **Enter**.

Change to a different drive

Oops!
If you see the message
Not ready reading
drive A Abort, Retry,
Fail?, you may not have
inserted a disk into the
drive or you may not have
inserted the disk properly.
Insert a disk and
type R to retry.

1. **Insert a formatted disk into drive A.**

   You may have just one floppy disk drive. If so, it is drive A. If you have more than one drive, drive A is usually the top drive of the computer.

   For help with this step, see *TASK: Insert a 5 1/4-inch disk* or *TASK: Insert a 3 1/2-inch disk* (depending on the size of your disk drive).

   A formatted disk is a disk that has been prepared for use. If you need to format a disk, see *Easy DOS* or *Using MS-DOS 5*.

2. **Type A:.**

   Typing A: specifies the drive that you want to change to (drive A). The name of a drive consists of two parts: the letter and a colon. Be sure not to insert a space between the two items.

3. **Press Enter.**

   Pressing Enter confirms the command. You see A:\> on-screen. This prompt reminds you that drive A is the current drive.

   To change back to drive C, type C: and press Enter.

```
C:\>A:
A:\>
```

after

1. Insert a disk into the drive.

2. Type the drive letter followed by a colon (such as **A:**, **B:**, or **C:**).

3. Press **Enter**.

To change to a different drive

Why change drives?
You need to change
drives when you want to
access files on another
drive. For instance, you
may want to copy the files
on the disk in drive A to
drive C (or vice versa).
You also may want to
display the files on the
disk in drive A.

Copy a file

before

```
C:\>COPY AUTOEXEC.BAT AUTOEXEC.OLD
```

1. Type **CD** and press **Enter**.

   This step changes to the root directory. For help with this step, see *TASK: Change to the root directory*.

2. Type **COPY**.

   The COPY command tells DOS to make a copy of the file.

3. Press the **space bar once**.

   This step inserts a space between the command name and the next part of the command (the file name).

4. Type **AUTOEXEC.BAT**.

   After you type the COPY command, you type the name of the file you want to copy. In this case, you are copying the AUTOEXEC.BAT file.

5. Press the **space bar once**.

   This step inserts a space between the file name and the next part of the command (the file name for the new file).

6. Type **AUTOEXEC.OLD**.

   AUTOEXEC.OLD is the name you want to assign the copy of the file. The total command is COPY AUTOEXEC.BAT AUTOEXEC.OLD. This command makes a copy of the file AUTOEXEC.BAT and names the file AUTOEXEC.OLD.

   Be sure that you haven't used the name AUTOEXEC.OLD for another file. If you have, be sure that you don't need the other AUTOEXEC.OLD file. This procedure will overwrite any data that was in that file.

Easy **PC**

```
C:\>COPY AUTOEXEC.BAT AUTOEXEC.OLD
        1 file(s) copied

C:\>DIR AUTOEXEC.*

 Volume in drive C is HARD DISK
 Volume Serial Number is 1724-0637
 Directory of C:\

AUTOEXEC OLD          98 09-04-91  12:49a
AUTOEXEC BAT          98 09-04-91  12:49a
        2 file(s)            196 bytes
                         2367488 bytes free


C:\>
```

after

Copy a file to another directory
To copy a file to another directory, see *TASK: Copy a file to another directory*.

7. **Press Enter**.

   Pressing Enter confirms the command. You see the message 1 file(s) copied. Now you have two versions of the same file, and each file has a different name. To confirm that a copy has been made, follow the next step.

8. Type **DIR AUTOEXEC.*** and press **Enter**.

   This command tells DOS to display all files with the file name AUTOEXEC, no matter what extension those files have. You see both the file named AUTOEXEC.BAT and the file named AUTOEXEC.OLD.

Start from the correct place
If you see the message File not found, the file name could not be found. Be sure that you are in the correct directory (the directory that contains the file). Try typing the command again.

REVIEW

1. Change to the directory that contains the file you want to copy.

2. Type **COPY**.

3. Press the **space bar once**.

4. Type the name of the file you want to copy.

5. Press the **space bar once**.

6. Type the file name for the copy. If necessary, first type the path and/or the drive letter.

7. Press **Enter**.

To copy a file

Copy a file to another directory

before

```
C:\>CD\

C:\>COPY AUTOEXEC.OLD C:\DATA
```

1. **Type CD\ and press Enter.**

   This step changes to the root directory. For help with this step, see *TASK: Change to the root directory*.

2. **Type COPY.**

   The COPY command tells DOS to make a copy of the file.

3. **Press the space bar once.**

   The space bar inserts a space between the command name and the next part of the command (the file name).

4. **Type AUTOEXEC.OLD.**

   After the COPY command, you type the name of the file you want to copy. In this case, the name of the file is AUTOEXEC.OLD.

5. **Press the space bar once.**

   The space bar inserts a space between the file name and the next part of the command (the directory for the new file).

6. **Type C:\DATA.**

   Typing C:\DATA tells DOS to place the copy in the directory C:\DATA. The file will have the same name. If you don't have this directory, use the name of one that you do have. If you want to create this directory, see *TASK: Make a directory*.

```
C:\>CD\

C:\>COPY AUTOEXEC.OLD C:\DATA
        1 file(s) copied

C:\>CD\DATA

C:\DATA>DIR

 Volume in drive C is HARD DISK
 Volume Serial Number is 1724-0637
 Directory of C:\DATA

.             <DIR>      09-04-91  12:39a
..            <DIR>      09-04-91  12:39a
AUTOEXEC OLD        98 09-04-91  12:49a
        3 file(s)        98 bytes
                     2326528 bytes free

C:\DATA>
```

after

Use a different file name
You can name the file something different by typing the new file name after you type the path in step 6.

7. Press **Enter**.

Pressing Enter confirms the command. You see the message
`1 file(s) copied`. Now you have two versions of the same file: one in the root directory and one in the DATA directory.

The After screen shows the contents of the DATA directory. You see AUTOEXEC.OLD

REVIEW

To copy a file to another directory

1. Change to the directory that contains the file you want to copy.

2. Type **COPY**.

3. Press the **space bar once**.

4. Type the name of the file you want to copy.

5. Press the **space bar once**.

6. Type the path—the directory where you want to store the copy. If you want to name the file something different from the original name, type the path and the new file name.

7. Press **Enter**.

Rename a file

before

```
C:\DATA>RENAME AUTOEXEC.OLD AUTOEXEC.BAK
```

1. **Type CD\DATA and press Enter.**
   This command tells DOS to change to the DATA directory. This directory contains the file that you want to rename.

2. **Type RENAME.**
   RENAME is the command that you use to rename files.

3. **Press the space bar once.**
   Pressing the space bar inserts a space between the command name and the next part of the command (the name of the file you want to rename).

4. **Type AUTOEXEC.OLD.**
   AUTOEXEC.OLD is the name of the file that you want to rename. If you don't have this file, use one that you do have.

5. **Press the space bar once.**
   Pressing the space bar inserts a space between the file name and the next part of the command (the new name you want to assign the file).

6. **Type AUTOEXEC.BAK.**
   AUTOEXEC.BAK is the new name you want to assign the file.

7. **Press Enter.**
   Pressing Enter confirms the command. The file named AUTOEXEC.OLD is now named AUTOEXEC.BAK.

Easy **PC**

```
C:\DATA>RENAME AUTOEXEC.OLD AUTOEXEC.BAK

C:\DATA>DIR

 Volume in drive C is HARD DISK
 Volume Serial Number is 1724-0637
 Directory of C:\DATA

.            <DIR>       09-04-91   12:39a
..           <DIR>       09-04-91   12:39a
AUTOEXEC BAK          98 09-04-91   12:49a
AUTOEXEC BAT          98 09-04-91   12:49a
Q        BAT         128 08-28-91   12:01a
WS4      BAT         128 08-28-91   12:02a
        6 file(s)         452 bytes
                      2220032 bytes free

C:\DATA>
```

after

8. Type **DIR** and press **Enter**.

   This step displays a directory listing so that you can verify that the file was renamed.

1. Change to the directory that contains the file you want to rename.

2. Type **RENAME**.

3. Press the **space bar once**.

4. Type the name of the file you want to rename.

5. Press the **space bar once**.

6. Type the new name you want to assign the file.

7. Press **Enter**.

Name a group of files
You also can rename a group of files by using *wild cards*. For information on using wild cards, see *Easy DOS* or *Using MS-DOS 5*.

To rename a file

Why rename a file?
Rename a file when the original file name is not descriptive of the file's contents.

Delete a file

```
C:\DATA>DEL AUTOEXEC.BAK
```

Oops!
If you see the message
File not found, the file
name you typed does not
exist. Check your typing
and try again.

1. Type **CD\DATA** and press **Enter**.

   This step tells DOS to change to the DATA directory. This directory contains the file you want to delete.

2. Type **DEL**.

   The DEL command tells DOS to delete a file.

3. Press the **space bar once**.

   The space bar inserts a space between the command name and the next part of the command (the file name).

4. Type **AUTOEXEC.BAK**.

   After the DEL command, you type the name of the file you want to delete. In this case, the name of the file is AUTOEXEC.BAK. (If you don't have this file, type the name of one you do have—one that you want to delete.)

   Be sure that you want to delete the file you specify in this step.

5. Press **Enter**.

   Pressing Enter confirms the command. The file you specified is deleted.

6. Type **DIR** and press **Enter**.

   This step displays a directory listing so that you can verify the file was deleted.

```
C:\DATA>DEL AUTOEXEC.BAK

C:\DATA>DIR

 Volume in drive C is HARD DISK
 Volume Serial Number is 1724-0637
 Directory of C:\DATA

.              <DIR>      09-04-91  12:39a
..             <DIR>      09-04-91  12:39a
AUTOEXEC BAT       98 09-04-91  12:49a
Q        BAT      128 08-28-91  12:01a
WS4      BAT      128 08-28-91  12:02a
        5 file(s)        354 bytes
                     2195456 bytes free

C:\DATA>
```

after

1. Change to the directory that contains the file you want to delete.

2. Type **DEL**.

3. Press the **space bar once**.

4. Type the name of the file you want to delete.

5. Press **Enter**.

Be careful!
It is easy to type DEL when you mean to type something else. Be sure to read all prompts carefully. Also, you should use the DIR command to review the file listing of the disk or directory before you delete a file.

To delete a file

Why delete a file?
Delete a file that you no longer need. Storing files on disk takes up space. You will quickly run out of space on the hard disk if you don't periodically delete files that you no longer need.

Working with DOS

Delete all files

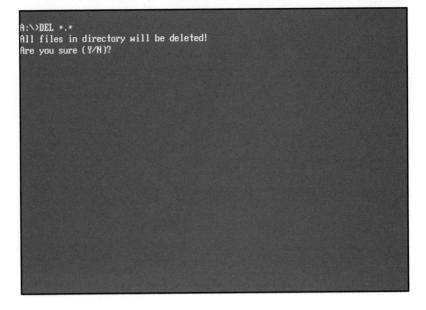

```
A:\>DEL *.*
All files in directory will be deleted!
Are you sure (Y/N)?
```

Oops!
If you change your mind, type N for step 7 of the Task section.

1. **Insert a disk into drive A.**

   Insert a disk that contains files you do not need. Do not insert a disk that contains files you want to save.

   For help with inserting a disk, see *TASK: Insert a 5 1/4-inch disk* or *TASK: Insert a 3 1/2-inch disk*, depending on the size of your floppy disk drive.

2. **Type A: and press Enter.**

   This command tells DOS to switch to drive A. Drive A contains the files that you want to delete.

   To delete files in a directory, change to that directory for this step.

3. **Type DEL.**

   The DEL command tells DOS to delete a file.

4. **Press the space bar once.**

   The space bar inserts a space between the command name and the next part of the command (the file name).

5. **Type *.*.**

   After the DEL command, you type the name of the file that you want to delete. The wild cards used here (*.*) tell DOS that you want to delete all files.

   Be sure that you want to delete all files before you type this command.

Easy **PCs**

```
A:\>DEL *.*
All files in directory will be deleted!
Are you sure (Y/N)?Y

A:\>DIR

 Volume in drive A is DATA DISK
 Volume Serial Number is 07E9-1C5B
 Directory of A:\

File not found

A:\>
```

after

Be careful!
It is easy to type DEL
when you mean to type
something else. Be sure
to read all prompts
carefully. Also, you
should use the DIR
command to review the
file listing of the disk or
directory before you
delete a file.

6. Press **Enter**.

   Pressing Enter confirms the command. You see the message All files in directory will be deleted! Are you sure (Y/N)?

7. Type **Y** and press **Enter**.

   This step confirms the deletion. All files are deleted.

8. Type **DIR** and press **Enter**.

   This step displays a directory listing so that you can confirm that the files were deleted.

REVIEW

To delete all files

1. Change to the drive or directory that contains the files you want to delete.

2. Type **DEL**.

3. Press the **space bar once**.

4. Type *.*.

5. Press **Enter**.

6. Type **Y**.

7. Press **Enter**.

Remove a directory

before

```
C:\>RD\DATA
```

1. **From the root directory, type RD.**

   RD is the remove directory command. For help changing to the root directory, see *TASK: Change to the root directory*.

2. **Type \DATA.**

   DATA is the name of the directory that you want to remove. The entire command is RD\DATA. (If you don't have a directory named DATA, type the name of one that you do have. Make sure that it is a directory you no longer need.)

3. **Press Enter.**

   Pressing Enter confirms the command. The directory is removed.

4. **Type DIR and press Enter.**

   This step displays a directory listing so that you can verify that the directory is removed.

```
Volume in drive C is HARD DISK
Volume Serial Number is 1724-0637
Directory of C:\

HARDCARD      <DIR>       09-04-91  12:10a
DOS           <DIR>       05-18-91  12:16a
CONFIG   SYS        74  09-04-91  12:49a
OLD_DOS  1    <DIR>       09-04-91  12:39a
WINA20   386      9349  04-09-91   5:00a
AUTOEXEC BAT        98  09-04-91  12:49a
TREEINFO NCD       299  09-04-91  12:18a
FRECOVER DAT     38912  09-04-91  12:00a
FRECOVER BAK     38912  09-04-91  12:00a
COLLAGE       <DIR>       08-28-91  12:01a
WORD5         <DIR>       05-18-91  12:03a
NU            <DIR>       05-18-91  12:17a
CHOICE        <DIR>       05-18-91  12:20a
WP51          <DIR>       05-18-91  12:23a
COMMAND  COM     47845  04-09-91   5:00a
QPRO          <DIR>       06-24-91   2:46a
       16 file(s)      135489 bytes
                      2621440 bytes free

C:\>
```

after

1. Type **RD**.

2. Press the **space bar once**.

3. Type the name of the directory that you want to remove.

4. Press **Enter**.

To remove a directory

Delete all files
Before you remove a directory, you must delete all files in that directory. The directory in this example (DATA) didn't contain any files. If it did, you would see an error message. In this case, delete all files. (See *TASK: Delete all files*.) Then try this task again.

Try this tip
If you have trouble removing a directory, the directory may contain other directories. When you type DEL *.*, you delete all the files, but you don't remove the directories. You must use the RD (remove directory) command to remove the directories within any directory.

Working with DOS

Start a DOS program

before

```
C:\>CD\WORD55

C:\WORD55>
```

1. **Type CD\WORD55.**

   CD is the change directory command. To start a program, you first move to the directory that contains the program files. This step tells DOS to change to the WORD55 directory. If you don't have this directory, type the name of one you do have—one that contains a program.

2. **Press Enter.**

   This step changes to the WORD55 directory. You see the prompt C:\WORD55>. The Before screen shows this step.

3. **Type WORD.**

   WORD is the command to start the program. In this case, you start Microsoft Word, which is a word processor. If you don't have this program, type the name of a program you do have. If you don't know the name, check the application manual.

4. **Press Enter.**

   Pressing Enter confirms the command; the program is started.

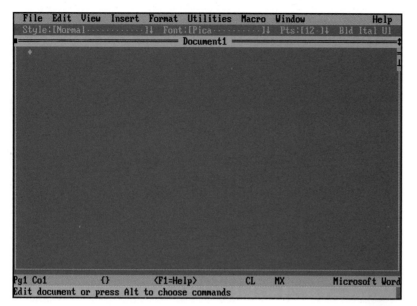

```
 File  Edit  View  Insert  Format  Utilities  Macro  Window            Help
 Style:[Normal···············]↓  Font:[Pica············]↓  Pts:[12·]↓  Bld Ital Ul
════════════════════════════════ Document1 ════════════════════════════════
 ◆
                                                                              │

















Pg1 Co1          {}          <F1=Help>          CL    MX        Microsoft Word
Edit document or press Alt to choose commands
```

after

REVIEW

Try this tip
If you don't know the file name for the program, type DIR *.EXE and press Enter. When the directory list is displayed, check to see whether any names look familiar. Program files usually have the extension EXE and are usually shortened versions of the program name.

1. Change to the directory that contains the program.

2. Type the command that starts the program. Here are some common program names:

Harvard Graphics	HG
Lotus 1-2-3	123
Q&A	QA
Quattro Pro	Q
Quicken	Q
Windows	WIN
Word	WORD
WordPerfect	WP
WordStar	WS

3. Press Enter.

Skip changing directories
Some programs are set up so that you don't have to change to the directory. You can just type the command name from anywhere to start the program. Check your application manual; look for information on adding the program to the PATH command.

Exit a DOS program

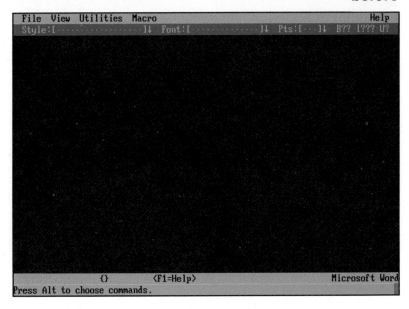

Oops!
If you cannot figure out
how to exit, check the
application manual.

1. **Start the program.**

    For help with this step, see *TASK: Start a DOS program*. This task
    uses Microsoft Word as an example. Depending on the program,
    you will have to follow a different procedure to exit.

2. **Press Alt.**

    This step accesses the menu bar so that you can make a menu
    selection.

3. **Press F.**

    This step opens the File menu. You see a list of File commands.

4. **Press x.**

    This step selects the Exit command and exits the program.

    Each program works differently. Here are some tips on exiting:

    Look for an Exit command on the File menu. Or look for a Quit or
    Exit menu.

    Try pressing the Esc key. Pressing this key may exit the program or
    display information that explains how to exit.

    Check the application manual.

Easy PC

```
C:\WORD55>
```

after

1. Open the **File** menu.

2. Select the **Exit** command.

Save your work
If you have been working in an application, save your work before you exit. Otherwise, you will lose your work.

To exit a DOS program

Working with Microsoft Windows

This section includes the following tasks:

Start Microsoft Windows

Select a menu command

Exit Microsoft Windows

Get help for Microsoft Windows

Open a window

Close a window

Select a window

Maximize a window

Restore a window

Minimize a window

Move a window

Resize a window

Start a Microsoft Windows program

Exit a Microsoft Windows program

Start Microsoft Windows

before

C:\>

Oops!
To exit Microsoft Windows, see *TASK: Exit Microsoft Windows.*

1. **From the DOS prompt, type win.**

   If you don't see the DOS prompt on-screen, you need to start your computer. See *TASK: Turn on computer*. Win is the command to start Microsoft Windows.

2. **Press Enter.**

   Pressing Enter starts the program. You see the Program Manager in a window on-screen. The Program Manager is an application that comes with Microsoft Windows.

   The Program Manager window includes many different elements—menu bar, title bar, icons, and so on. See the Basics part of this book for a description of these elements.

   Your screen may look different from the After screen. You can rearrange the desktop (move the icons, open windows, and so on). Microsoft Windows remembers how your desktop looked the last time you used Microsoft Windows. When you start Microsoft Windows again, you see this same layout. Also, you may have different group windows (sets of programs) on-screen, depending on what programs you have installed and what changes you have made.

after

Change the desktop
You can change how the
desktop appears—open
windows, rearrange
windows, size windows,
and so on. See the tasks
in this section.

REVIEW

1. From the DOS prompt, type **win**.

2. Press **Enter**.

To start Microsoft Windows

Select a menu command

before

Oops!
To close a menu without making a selection, click on the menu name in the menu bar. You also can press the Esc key.

1. **Point to File in the menu bar and click the left mouse button.**

   This step opens the File menu. You see a list of File commands.

2. **Point to Exit Windows and click the left mouse button.**

   This step chooses the Exit command. On-screen you see the Exit Windows dialog box. This box reminds you that you are exiting Microsoft Windows.

3. **Point to OK and click the left mouse button.**

   This step confirms that you do want to exit. You return to DOS.

```
C:\>
```

after

1. Click on the menu name in the menu bar.

2. Click on the command.

What do the ellipses mean?
Some commands are followed by ellipses (...). This means that you must specify additional options before you execute the command. See *Easy Windows,* 3.1 Edition, or *Using Windows 3.1,* Special Edition, for information on dialog boxes.

Try a shortcut
Some menu commands have shortcut keys. You can execute the command by pressing the shortcut key. Shortcut keys are listed on the menu.

Exit Microsoft Windows

before

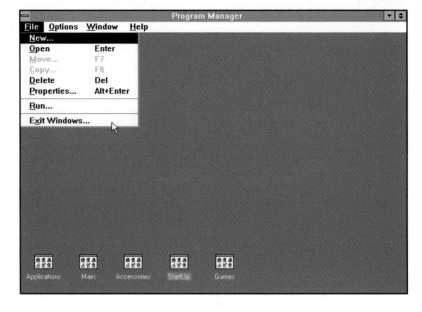

Oops!
If you don't want to quit Microsoft Windows, click on Cancel for step 3.

1. **Point to File in the menu bar and click the left mouse button.**

   This step opens the File menu. You see a list of File commands.

2. **Point to Exit Windows and click the left mouse button.**

   This step chooses the Exit command. On-screen you see the Exit Windows dialog box. This box reminds you that you are exiting the program.

3. **Point to OK and click the left mouse button.**

   This step confirms that you do want to exit. You return to DOS.

C:\>

after

Restart Microsoft Windows
To restart Microsoft Windows, see *TASK: Start Microsoft Windows.*

To exit Microsoft Windows

1. Click on **File** in the menu bar.

2. Click on the **Exit Windows** command.

3. Click on the **OK** button.

Try a shortcut
As a shortcut for steps 1 and 2, double-click the Control menu box.

Get help for Microsoft Windows

before

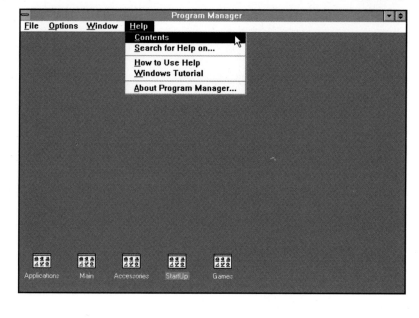

Oops!
To close the Help window quickly, double-click on the Control menu box.

1. Point to **Help** in the menu bar and click the left mouse button.

   This step opens the Help menu. On-screen you see a list of Help menu options.

2. Point to **Contents** and click the left mouse button.

   This step chooses the Contents command. The Help window for the Program Manager opens.

   Microsoft Windows offers many ways to get help, and the Help feature has its own menu system. For complete information on all Help options, see *Using Microsoft Windows 3.1,* Special Edition.

3. Point to **Arrange Windows and Icons** and click the left mouse button.

   This step chooses the topic. When the mouse pointer is on a topic for which you can get help, the pointer changes to a hand with a pointing finger. You see an explanation of how to arrange windows and icons.

   To close the Help window, follow steps 4 and 5.

4. Point to the **Control menu box** and click the left mouse button.

   Remember that the Control menu box is the small bar to the left of the window's title bar. Clicking on this box displays the Control menu.

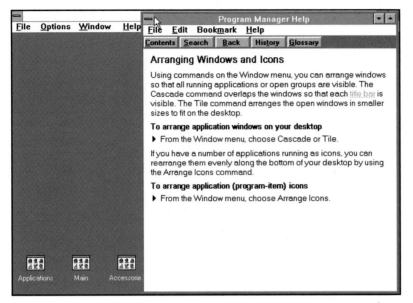

after

5. Point to **Close** and click the left mouse button.

This step closes the Help window.

1. Click on **Help** in the menu bar.

2. Click on the **Contents** command.

3. Click on the topic you want.

4. Click on the **Control menu box** when you want to close the Help window.

5. Click on the **Close** button.

To get help for Microsoft Windows

Scroll the Help screen
To scroll through the Help window, click on the scroll arrow on the right side of the window.

Try a shortcut
Press the F1 key as a shortcut for steps 1 and 2 of the Task section.

Open a window

before

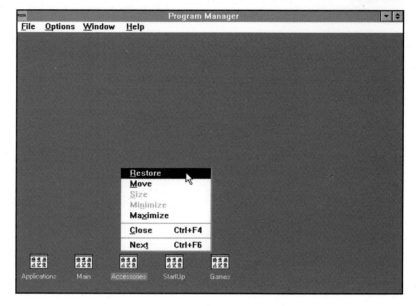

Oops!
To close the window, see
TASK: Close a window.

1. **Point to the Accessories icon and click the left mouse button.**

   All programs are stored in group windows. A group window is indicated by a group icon. The name of the group window appears under the group icon and is highlighted when you click on the icon.

   This step opens the Control menu for this window. You use this menu to manipulate the program window (restore, move, size, close, and so on).

2. **Point to Restore and click the left mouse button.**

   This step tells Microsoft Windows to restore or open the group window. The Accessories window appears. You see various accessory programs—Calculator, Calendar, and so on. These programs are provided with Microsoft Windows.

   Note that your window may appear in a different location and size than the one in the After screen. Microsoft Windows remembers the location and size of the window from the last time it was opened. The window is then "restored" to how it appeared the last time you exited Microsoft Windows. You can move and resize the window so that it is placed where you want it. See the tasks in this section for more information.

Easy **PCs**

after

Open other windows
You can open more than one window at a time. To do so, follow this same procedure. Use the other tasks in this section to arrange the windows on-screen.

REVIEW

1. Point to the window icon and click the left mouse button.

2. Click on the **Restore** command.

To open a window

Try a shortcut
To open a window quickly, double-click on the icon of the window you want to open.

Close a window

before

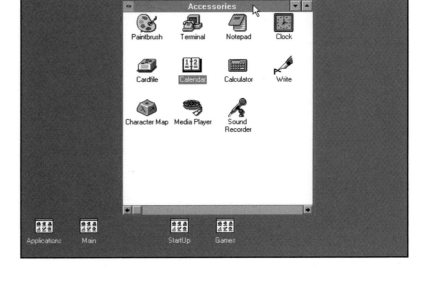

Oops!
Be sure to click on the Control menu box for the window you want to close. The Program Manager also has a Control menu box. If you click on this menu box, you see the Exit Windows dialog box. If this happens, click on Cancel.

1. **Open the Accessories window.**

   To open the window, point to the Accessories icon and double-click the left mouse button. (*Double-click* means to press the mouse button twice in rapid succession.) For more information, see *TASK: Open a window*.

2. **Point to the Control menu box and click the left mouse button.**

   Remember that the Control menu box is the little bar to the left of the window's title bar. Clicking on this box displays the Control menu.

3. **Point to Close and click the left mouse button.**

   This step chooses the Close command. The window is closed and restored to an icon.

   Your desktop can get confusing with different windows of varying sizes open. If you start getting confused, close all windows and then open just those windows that you need.

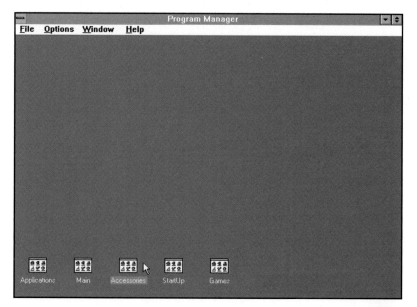

after

Try a shortcut
To close a window
quickly, double-click on
the Control menu box.

1. Click on the Control menu box.

2. Click on the Close command.

To close a window

Try a keyboard shortcut
To use the keyboard to
close a window quickly,
press the Ctrl-F4 key
combination.

Select a window

before

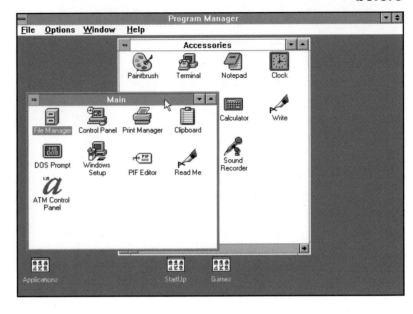

Oops!
Follow this same procedure to change to a different window.

1. **Open the Accessories window.**

   To open the window, point to the Accessories icon and double-click the left mouse button. For more information, see *TASK: Open a window*.

2. **Open the Main window.**

   To open this window, point to the Main icon and double-click the left mouse button. For more information, see *TASK: Open a window*.

   You now have two windows open on-screen. The window you just opened is the current or active window. You can tell which window is active by looking at the border and the title bar. An active window has a colored border and title bar. (The title bar is the top line of the window and includes the name of the window. The border is the edge of the window.)

   The Before screen shows this step.

3. **Point to Window in the menu bar and click the left mouse button.**

   This step opens the Window menu. You see a list of numbered windows. The current window (Main) has a check mark next to it.

Easy **PCs**

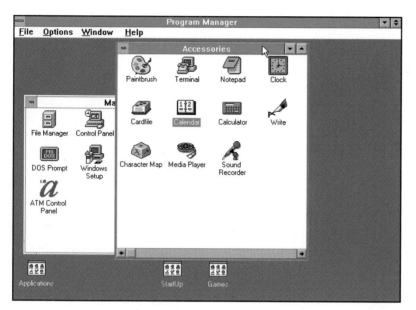

after

Try a shortcut
If you can see the window you want on-screen, you can point anywhere on that window and click the left mouse button to select the window quickly. (You can move and size the window, if necessary, to see all the windows.)

4. Point to **Accessories** and click the left mouse button.

   This step selects the Accessories window from the Window menu. This window moves to the top of the desktop and becomes the active window. The border and title bar both appear in a different color.

REVIEW

1. Click on **Window** in the menu bar.

2. In the list that appears, click on the name of the window that you want to select.

To select a window

Maximize a window

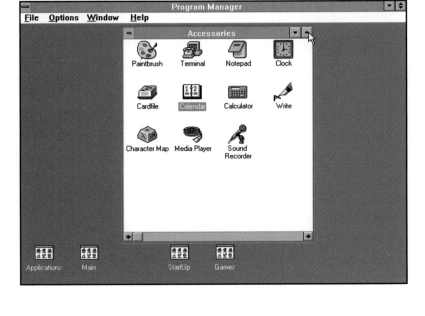

Oops!
To restore the window to the previous size, see *TASK: Restore a window.*

1. **Open the Accessories window.**

   To open the window, point to the Accessories icon and double-click the left mouse button. For more information, see *TASK: Open a window.*

2. **Point to the Control menu box and click the left mouse button.**

   Remember that the Control menu box is the little bar in the title bar of the window. Clicking on this menu box displays the Control menu.

3. **Point to Maximize and click the left mouse button.**

   Clicking on Maximize chooses the Maximize command. The window fills the Program Manager screen. You see Program Manager-[Accessories] in the title bar; this is the name of the window.

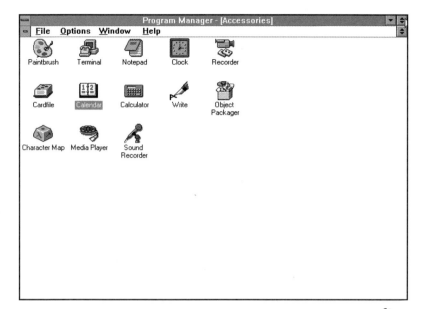

Program Manager - [Accessories]

File   Options   Window   Help

Paintbrush   Terminal   Notepad   Clock   Recorder

Cardfile   Calendar   Calculator   Write   Object Packager

Character Map   Media Player   Sound Recorder

after

Try a shortcut
To maximize a window quickly, click on the Maximize button in the title bar. The Maximize button is an up arrow.

REVIEW

1. Click on the **Control menu box** for the window.

2. Click on the **Maximize** command.

To maximize a window

Maximize, Minimize, and Restore
Keep in mind the differences between Maximize, Minimize, and Restore. Maximize expands the window so that it fills the entire screen. Minimize returns the window to an icon. Restore returns the window to its last size and location.

Restore a window

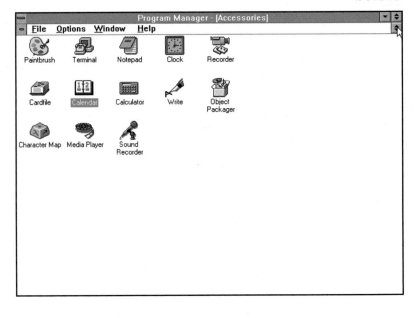

Oops!
You cannot restore a window unless it has been maximized or minimized.

1. **Open the Accessories window.**

   To open the window, point to the Accessories icon and double-click the left mouse button. For more information, see *TASK: Open a window*.

   You use Restore after you have maximized or minimized the window. For this example, you will maximize the window.

2. **Point to the Control menu box and click the left mouse button.**

   This step opens the Control menu.

3. **Point to Maximize and click the left mouse button.**

   This step chooses the Maximize command. The window expands to fill the Program Manager screen. Now that the window is maximized, you can restore it to its original size.

   The Before screen shows this step.

4. **Point to the Control menu box for the Accessories window and click the left mouse button.**

   This step opens the Control menu. Be sure to click on the menu box next to the menu bar. The top Control menu box is for the Program Manager window; you do not want to change the Program Manager window.

Easy **PCs**

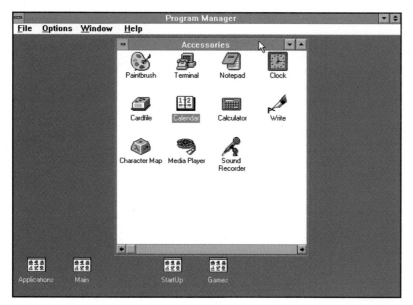

after

5. Point to **Restore** and click the left mouse button.

   This step chooses the Restore command. The window is restored to its original size and location.

1. Maximize or minimize the window.

2. Click on the **Control menu box**.

3. Click on the **Restore** command.

Try a shortcut
To quickly restore a window that has been maximized, click on the Restore button in the title bar. The Restore button is a two-headed (up and down) arrow.

Maximize, Minimize, and Restore
Keep in mind the differences between Maximize, Minimize, and Restore. Maximize expands the window so that it fills the entire screen. Minimize returns the window to an icon. Restore returns the window to its last size and location.

To restore a window

Minimize a window

before

Oops!
To restore the window,
see *TASK: Restore a window.*

1. **Open the Accessories window.**

   To open the window, point to the Accessories icon and double-click the left mouse button. For more information, see *TASK: Open a window.*

2. **Point to the Control menu box and click the left mouse button.**

   Remember that the Control menu box is the little bar in the title bar. Clicking on this menu box displays the Control menu.

3. **Point to Minimize and click the left mouse button.**

   This step chooses the Minimize command. The window is restored to an icon.

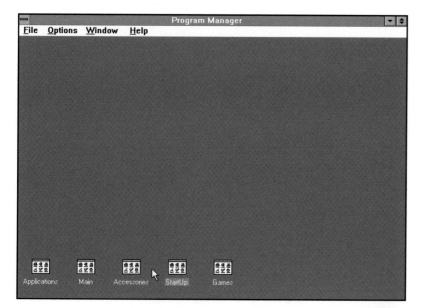

| Program Manager | ▼ ‡ |
| File Options Window Help | |

Applications   Main   Accessories   StartUp   Games

after

Try a shortcut
To minimize a window quickly, click on the Minimize button in the title bar. The Minimize button is a down arrow.

1. Click on the **Control menu box** of the window you want to minimize.

2. Click on the **Minimize** command.

To minimize a window

Maximize, Minimize, and Restore
Keep in mind the differences between Maximize, Minimize, and Restore. Maximize expands the window so that it fills the entire screen. Minimize returns the window to an icon. Restore returns the window to its last size and location.

Move a window

before

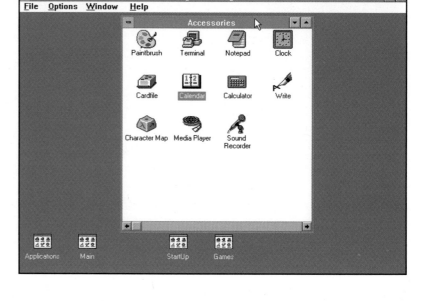

Oops!
If the window does not move, you may not have placed the mouse pointer in the correct spot. If you click on the border of the window, you resize the window instead of moving it. Be sure to point to the title bar.

1. **Open the Accessories window.**

    To open the window, point to the Accessories icon and double-click the left mouse button. For more information, see *TASK: Open a window*.

2. **Point to the title bar.**

    The title bar displays the window name. Be sure to point to the title bar—not the window border. Pointing to the window border resizes the window rather than moves it.

3. **Press and hold down the left mouse button.**

    When you press and hold down the mouse button, the window border turns a lighter shade.

4. **Drag up and to the right until the window is in the upper right corner of the screen.**

    As you drag, you see the outline of the window.

5. **Release the mouse button.**

    When you release the mouse button, the window moves to the new location.

    If you exit the program with windows open, Microsoft Windows remembers the size and location of any open windows.

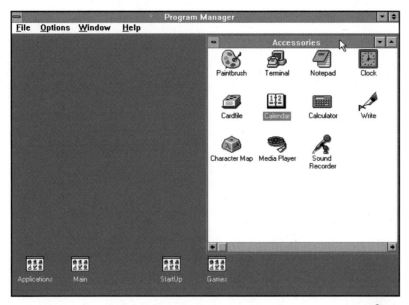

after

1. Open the window you want to move. If the window is open, select the window. See *TASK: Open a window* and *TASK: Select a window*.

2. Point to the title bar.

3. Press and hold down the mouse button and drag the window to the new location.

4. Release the mouse button.

To move a window

Working with Microsoft Windows

Resize a window

before

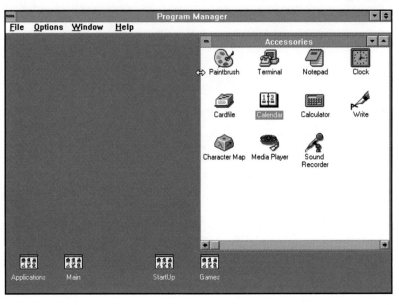

1. **Open the Accessories window.**

   To open the window, point to the Accessories icon and double-click the left mouse button. For more information, see *TASK: Open a window*.

2. **Move the mouse pointer to the left border.**

   You must place the mouse pointer exactly on the border. When the pointer is in the correct spot, it changes to a two-headed arrow.

3. **Press and hold down the left mouse button.**

   When you press and hold down the mouse button, the border turns a lighter shade.

4. **Drag to the left until the window stretches to the left edge of the screen.**

   As you drag, you see the outline of the window border.

5. **Release the mouse button.**

   When you release the mouse button, the window is resized.

   If you exit the program with windows open, Microsoft Windows remembers the size and arrangement of the windows. The size and arrangement will be the same the next time you start Microsoft Windows.

Easy **PCs**

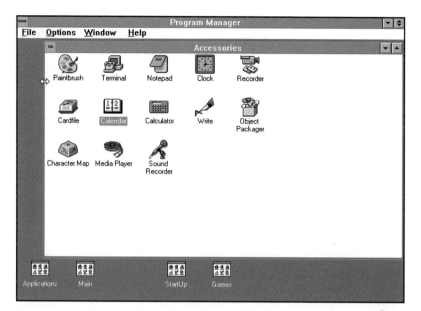

after

Resize other sides
You can resize the window from the left, right, top, or bottom. Just point to the border you want to move, press and hold down the mouse button, and then drag the border to the new spot.

1. Open the window you want to resize. If the window is open, select the window. See *TASK: Open a window* and *TASK: Select a window*.

2. Move the mouse pointer to the border that you want to move.

3. Press and hold down the mouse button and drag the border to the new location.

4. Release the mouse button.

To resize a window

Arrange all windows
If many windows are open on-screen and you want to see all of them, use the Arrange command on the Window menu. This command automatically sizes and moves windows so that they are all displayed.

Start a Microsoft Windows program

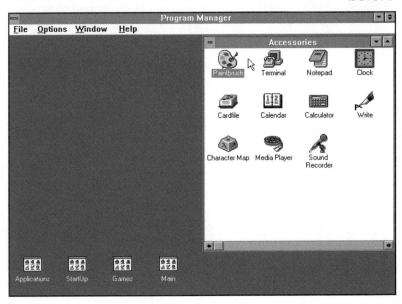

before

1. **Close all group windows so that only the program group icons are displayed.**

   You don't have to follow this step, but doing so enables you to find the group icon that you need. For help with this step, see *TASK: Close a window.*

2. **Double-click on the Accessories group icon.**

   This step opens the Accessories program window, as shown in the Before screen. Microsoft Windows comes with several accessory programs. These programs appear in the Accessories window.

3. **Double-click on the Paintbrush icon.**

   This step starts the Paintbrush program. Paintbrush is a draw program. You see a blank document window on-screen. For information on using Paintbrush, see *Using Windows 3.1,* Special Edition.

   There are many ways to run a program, and there are many programs that you can run from within Microsoft Windows (besides those supplied with the program). You also can run more than one program at a time. For complete information on program management, see *Using Windows 3.1,* Special Edition.

Easy **PCs**

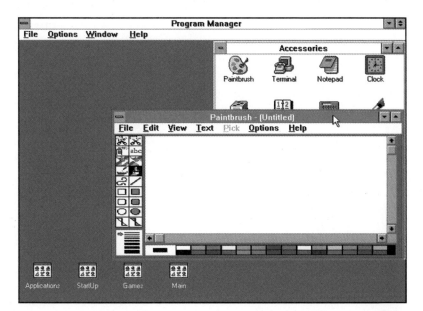

after

Exit the program
To exit the program, see
*TASK: Exit a Microsoft
Windows program.*

REVIEW

1. Open the group window that contains the program.

2. Double-click on the program icon to start the program.

**To start a
Microsoft
Windows
program**

Working with Microsoft Windows

Exit a Microsoft Windows program

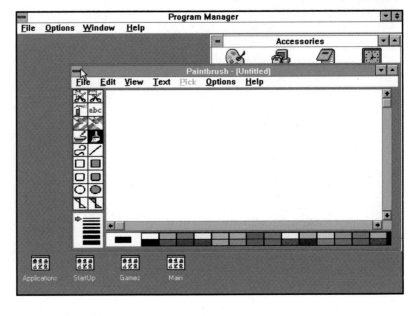

Oops!
To restart the program, see *TASK: Start a Microsoft Windows program.*

1. **Start the Paintbrush program.**

   To start Paintbrush, open the Accessories program group and then double-click the Paintbrush icon. For help with this step, see *TASK: Start a Microsoft Windows program*.

2. **Click on File in the menu bar.**

   This step opens the File menu. You see a list of File commands.

3. **Click on Exit.**

   This step selects the Exit command and closes the program. The Accessories window is still open on-screen.

   This procedure should work for most Microsoft Windows programs.

Easy **PCs**

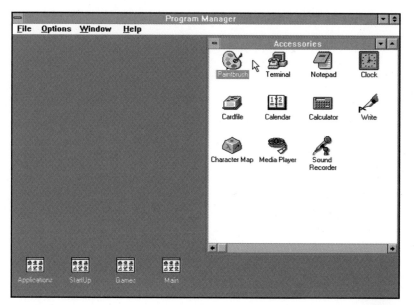

after

Try a shortcut
To exit a program quickly, double-click on the Control menu box for the program window.

1. Click on **File** in the menu bar.

2. Click on the **Exit** command.

To exit a Microsoft Windows program

Save your work
Be sure to save any of your work before you close the program. If you don't, the program will remind you that you need to save your work or you will lose it.

Using a Word Processing Program
(WordPerfect)

This section includes the following tasks:

Start a word processing program

Exit a word processing program

Get help

Type text

Add text

Insert a blank line

Delete a character

Select text

Delete text

Undelete text

Copy text

Move text

Make text bold

Save a document

Open a document

Start a word processing program

Oops!
To exit the program, see
*TASK: Exit a word
processing program.*

before

```
C:\>CD\WP51
C:\WP51>
```

1. **Turn on the computer and monitor.**

   For help with this task, see *TASK: Turn on the computer*. You should see the DOS prompt (C:\>) on-screen. To start the program, you have to tell DOS two things: where to find the program and the name of the program.

2. **Type CD\WP51.**

   This command tells DOS to change to the WP51 directory. (For information on changing directories, see *TASK: Change to a different directory*.) If your word processing program is stored in a different directory (has a different name), type that directory name rather than WP51.

   Some programs are set up so that you don't have to change to the directory. You can just type the command name from anywhere to start the program. Check your application manual; look for information on adding the program to the path.

3. **Press Enter.**

   This step confirms the command and places you in the WordPerfect directory. The Before screen shows this step.

4. **Type WP.**

   Typing WP tells DOS the name of the program. If you are using a different word processing program you will need to type a different command—a command for that program.

Doc 1 Pg 1 Ln 1" Pos 1"

after

Try this tip
If you don't know the name for the program, change to the directory that contains the program, type DIR *.EXE, and press Enter. When the directory list is displayed, check to see whether any names look familiar. Program files usually have the extension EXE and are usually shortened versions of the program name.

5. Press Enter.

This step executes the WP command and starts the program. You see the WordPerfect editing screen.

REVIEW

1. Turn on the computer and monitor.

2. Change to the directory that contains the program.

3. Type the program name and press Enter.

To start a word processing program

Use a different program?
The tasks in this section use WordPerfect as an example. You may use a different word processor, such as Microsoft Word or WordStar. Most word processors have the same capabilities as those listed in this section, although some steps may differ. See your application manual for more information.

Exit a word processing program

before

Save document? Yes (No)   (Text was not modified)

Oops!
To restart the program,
see *TASK: Start a word
processing program.*

1. **Press F7.**

   F7 is the Exit key in WordPerfect. You see the prompt Save document? Yes (No).

   If you are using another word processing program, check the manual for information on exiting the program. Exiting with the F7 key is unique to WordPerfect.

2. **Type N.**

   This step tells WordPerfect that you do not want to save the document. (If you do want to save the document—and most of the time you will—see *TASK: Save a document*.) You see the prompt Exit WP? No (Yes).

3. **Type Y.**

   This step tells WordPerfect that you do want to exit. You return to the DOS prompt.

C:\WP51>

after

Use a different program?
If you use a different word processing program, look for an Exit command in the File menu. Or try pressing the Esc key.

1. Press **F7** (Exit).

2. Type **N**. (If you want to save the file, see *TASK: Save a document.*)

3. Type **Y**.

To exit a word processing program

Get help

```
Help                                              WP 5.1   11/06/89

     Press any letter to get an alphabetical list of features.

          The list will include the features that start with that letter,
          along with the name of the key where the feature is found.  You
          can then press that key to get a description of how the feature
          works.


     Press any function key to get information about the use of the key.

          Some keys may let you choose from a menu to get more information
          about various options.  Press HELP again to display the template.












Selection: 0                                (Press ENTER to exit Help)
```

Oops!
To exit help, press Enter. You cannot press F1, F7, or Esc to exit help. Pressing these keys displays Help on that particular key.

1. **Press F3.**

   F3 is the Help key in WordPerfect. This step displays the opening Help screen, which explains how to use the help feature.

2. **Type M to get help on margins.**

   This step displays topics that start with the letter M. Margins - Left and Right appears halfway down the screen. The screen shows the name that WordPerfect has assigned to this key and the keys that you press to activate the feature.

3. **Press Enter.**

   This step exits the Help screen.

Easy **PCs**

```
Features [M]                    WordPerfect Key    Keystrokes

Macro Editor                    Macro Define       Ctrl-F10
Macro Commands                  Macro Commands     Ctrl-PgUp
Macro Commands, Help On         Macro Define       Ctrl-F10
Macros, Define                  Macro Define       Ctrl-F10
Macros, Execute                 Macro             Alt-F10
Macros, Keyboard Definition     Setup              Shft-F1,5
Mail Merge                      Merge/Sort         Ctrl-F9,1
Main Dictionary Location        Setup              Shft-F1,6,3
Manual Hyphenation              Format             Shft-F8,1,1
Map, Keyboard                   Setup              Shft-F1,5,8
Map Special Characters          Setup              Shft-F1,5
Margin Release                  Margin Release     Shft-Tab
Margins - Left and Right        Format             Shft-F8,1,7
Margins - Top and Bottom        Format             Shft-F8,2,5
Mark Text For Index (Block On)  Mark Text          Alt-F5,3
Mark Text For List (Block On)   Mark Text          Alt-F5,2
Mark Text For ToA (Block On)    Mark Text          Alt-F5,4
Mark Text For ToC (Block On)    Mark Text          Alt-F5,1
Master Document                 Mark Text          Alt-F5,2
Math                            Columns/Table      Alt-F7,3
More... Press m to continue.

Selection: 0                               (Press ENTER to exit Help)
```

after

1. Press **F3** (Help).

2. Type the first letter of the topic for which you want help.

3. Press **Enter** to exit help.

Use a different program?
Pressing F3 for help does not work in most software programs. Try pressing F1 to get help. F1 is the help key in many programs.

To get help

Type text

before

Doc 1 Pg 1 Ln 1" Pos 1"

Oops!
To delete text, see *TASK:
Delete text*.

Type the following text:

Typing in a word processing program is different from typing on a typewriter. You don't have to press the Return or Enter key when you reach the end of the line. The program automatically wraps words that won't fit to the next line.

This step enters text. As you type, you see the text on-screen. You can make corrections as you go. Press Backspace to delete any typos, and then type the correct character. For information on deleting text, see *TASK: Delete text*.

Note that you do not have to press Enter (Return) at the end of the line. WordPerfect moves text to the next line automatically. (This feature is called *word wrapping*.) On a typewriter, you cannot add or delete text in a certain line without retyping the entire line (or often, the entire document). With a word processing program, you can add or delete text and the program adjusts the lines automatically.

To move around the text (from character to character, word to word, and line to line), use the arrow keys ($\uparrow$, $\downarrow$, $\leftarrow$, or $\rightarrow$). Note that you cannot move past the end of the text.

Easy **PCs**

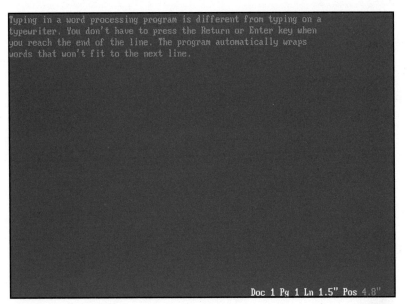

Typing in a word processing program is different from typing on a typewriter. You don't have to press the Return or Enter key when you reach the end of the line. The program automatically wraps words that won't fit to the next line.

Doc 1 Pg 1 Ln 1.5" Pos 4.8"

after

Insert a blank line
When you want to end a paragraph or insert a blank line, press Enter. See *TASK: Insert a blank line.*

R E V I E W

Type the text. Press **Enter** only at the end of the paragraph or when you want to insert a blank line.

To type text

Use a different program?
All word processing programs handle text in the same way. That is, just type the text!

Add text

before

It was a stormy night.

Doc 1 Pg 1 Ln 1" Pos 1.9"

Oops!
To delete text, see *TASK: Delete text.*

1. **Type It was a stormy night.**

   This step enters the text (as shown in the Before screen).

   For the rest of the tasks in this section, be sure to type any text shown in the Before screen.

2. **Use the arrow keys to move the cursor under the *s* in *stormy*.**

   After you have typed text, you can use the arrow keys to move around within the text. A flashing underline, called the *cursor*, indicates your position on-screen.

   This step places the cursor where you want to insert text.

3. **Type dark and.**

   This step inserts text and pushes existing text right. Note that you do not have to press the Ins key to Insert text. (Pressing the Ins key puts WordPerfect in Typeover mode, which means that every letter you type replaces an existing letter at the cursor's position. See *Easy WordPerfect* or *Using WordPerfect 5.1,* Special Edition, for information on this mode.)

4. **Press the space bar once.**

   This step inserts a space between the new text and the original text.

It was a dark and stormy night.

Doc 1 Pg 1 Ln 1" Pos 2.8"

after

1. Move the cursor to where you want to insert new text.

2. Type the text.

To add text

Text disappears?
If the text you type overwrites the original text, you are in Typeover mode. (You should see Typeover or a similar message on the last line of the screen.) Press Ins to turn off Typeover mode.

Use the mouse
Some programs let you use the mouse to move the cursor around on-screen. Use the mouse to place the pointer on-screen. Then click the mouse button.

Using a Word Processing Program

Insert a blank line

before

Dear Loretta:

Doc 1 Pg 1 Ln 1" Pos 2.3"

1. **Use the arrow keys to move the cursor to end of the line.**

   This step moves the cursor to the end of the line or paragraph.

   Be sure to type any text shown in the Before screen.

2. **Press Enter.**

   Pressing Enter ends the current paragraph and moves the cursor to the beginning of the next line.

3. **Press Enter.**

   Pressing Enter again inserts a blank line.

4. **Type How are you?**

   This step enters new text to the document. Notice that the new text is separated from the preceding text by a blank line.

Dear Loretta:

How are you?

Doc 1 Pg 1 Ln 1.33" Pos 2.2"

after

To insert a blank line

1. Move the cursor to the end of the paragraph.

2. Press **Enter twice**.

Delete a character

before

```
Chapterr






                                    Doc 1 Pg 1 Ln 1" Pos 1.7"
```

Oops!
To restore a deleted character, see *TASK: Undelete text*.

1. **Use the arrow keys to move the cursor under the last *r* in *Chapterr*.**

   This step places the cursor under the character that you want to delete.

   Remember to type any text shown in the Before screen.

2. **Press Del.**

   This step deletes the character. The word is now *Chapter*.

Easy **PCs**

Doc 1 Pg 1 Ln 1" Pos 1.7"

after

1. Move the cursor to the character to be deleted.

2. Press Del.

To delete a character

Use another method
You also can position the cursor to the right of the character that you want to delete and then press the Backspace key.

Use a different program?
These steps will work for most word processing programs.

Select text

before

```
Chapter 1




                                           Doc 1 Pg 1 Ln 1" Pos 1"
```

Oops!
To turn off Block mode,
press the Alt-F4 key
combination again.

1. Use the arrow keys to move the cursor to the *C* in
   Chapter.

   This step places the cursor under the first character that you want
   to select.

2. Press **Alt-F4**.

   Alt-F4 is the Block key combination. You see the message Block
   on flash in the lower left corner of the screen. This message
   reminds you that you are in Block mode.

3. Press the → key until you highlight the text *Chapter 1*.

   This step selects the text. After text is selected, you can copy it,
   move it, delete it, make it bold, and so on. Some of the other tasks
   in this section cover how to work with a block of selected text.

Easy **PCs**

Chapter 1

Block on   Doc 1 Pg 1 Ln 1" Pos 1.9"

after

To select text

1. Move the cursor to the first character that you want to select.

2. Press **Alt-F4** (Block).

3. Use the arrow keys to highlight the block.

Select text with a mouse
To select text with the mouse, click at the start of the text that you want to select. Hold down the mouse button, and then drag across the text you want to select. Release the mouse button.

Using a Word Processing Program

143

Delete text

before

Chapter 1
Chapter 1

Doc 1 Pg 1 Ln 1.17" Pos 1"

Oops!
To restore deleted text,
see *TASK: Undelete text*.

1. **Select the second line that reads *Chapter 1*.**

   This step selects the text that you want to delete. For help with selecting text, see *TASK: Select text*.

   Remember to type any text in the Before screen.

2. **Press Del.**

   Pressing the Del key tells WordPerfect to delete the text. Look at the lower left corner of the screen. You will see the prompt Delete Block? No (Yes).

3. **Type Y.**

   This step confirms that you want to delete the text; the text is deleted.

Chapter 1

Doc 1 Pg 1 Ln 1.17" Pos 1"

after

1. Select the text that you want to delete.

2. Press Del.

3. Type Y.

To delete text

Use a different program?
Most word processing programs do not ask you to confirm the deletion. If yours doesn't, skip step 3.

Try keyboard shortcuts
Most word processing programs offer keyboard shortcuts for deleting text. If you are using WordPerfect, for example, you can press the Ctrl-Backspace key combination to delete a word. See your application manual for information on shortcuts.

Undelete
text

```
Chapter 1
The Marriage Trifecta




                                    .




                                Doc 1 Pg 1 Ln 1.17" Pos 1"
```

Oops!
If you don't want to restore
the text, press the F1 key
for step 6 of the
Task section.

1. **Use the arrow keys to move the cursor under the *T* in *The*.**

   This step places the cursor at the start of the text that you want to delete. For this task, you will select some text, delete that text, and then restore it.

2. **Select the text *The Marriage Trifecta*.**

   Use the Alt-F4 key combination to select the text. See *TASK: Select text* for more information. This step selects the text to delete.

3. **Press Del.**

   Pressing the Del key tells WordPerfect to delete the text. Look in the lower left corner of the screen. You will see the prompt Delete Block? No (Yes).

4. **Type Y.**

   This step confirms that you want to delete the text; the text is deleted.

5. **Press F1.**

   F1 is the Cancel key. You see the prompt Undelete: 1 Restore; 2 Previous Deletion: 0. The text you just deleted appears again on-screen and is highlighted. The After screen shows this step.

```
Chapter 1
The Marriage Trifecta
```

```
Undelete: 1 Restore; 2 Previous Deletion: 0
```

after

6. Type **R**.

   This step selects Restore from the list of choices. The previously deleted text is restored at the cursor location.

1. Move the cursor to the spot where you want the restored text to appear.

2. Press **F1** (Cancel).

3. Type **R** to restore the text.

To undelete text

Restore other deletions
You can restore up to three previous sections of text. See *Using WordPerfect 5.1*, Special Edition, for more information.

Use a different program?
Pressing the F1 key in other word processing packages may not work. Look for an Undo command in the Edit menu or refer to your application manual.

Copy text

before

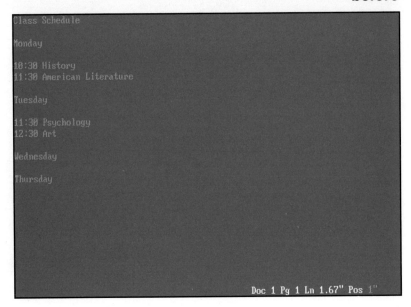

```
Class Schedule

Monday

10:30 History
11:30 American Literature

Tuesday

11:30 Psychology
12:30 Art

Wednesday

Thursday




                                                    Doc 1 Pg 1 Ln 1.67" Pos 1"
```

Oops!
To delete the copied text,
see *TASK: Delete text*.

1. **Use the arrow keys to move the cursor before the *10* in *10:30*.**

   This step places the cursor point at the start of the text you want to copy.

2. **Select the next three lines (the line that starts *10:30*, the line that starts *11:30*, and the next blank line).**

   To select text, use the Block key combination—Alt-F4. See *TASK: Select text* for help with this step.

3. **Press Ctrl-F4.**

   Ctrl-F4 is the Move key combination. You can move or copy text using this key combination. You see the prompt `Move: 1 Block; 2 Tabular Column; 3 Rectangle: 0`.

4. **Type B.**

   This step selects Block from the list of choices. You see the prompt `1 Move; 2 Copy; 3 Delete; 4 Append: 0`.

5. **Type C.**

   This step selects Copy from the list of choices.

6. **Use the arrow keys to move the cursor under the *T* in *Thursday*.**

   This step places the cursor where you want the copied text to appear. The copied text will appear before where the cursor is positioned.

Easy **PC**

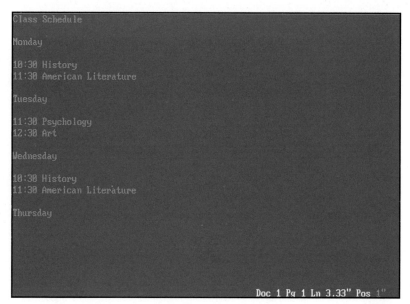

```
Class Schedule

Monday

10:30 History
11:30 American Literature

Tuesday

11:30 Psychology
12:30 Art

Wednesday

10:30 History
11:30 American Literature

Thursday


                                    Doc 1 Pg 1 Ln 3.33" Pos 1"
```

after

Use a different program?
The Ctrl-F4 key combination does not work in other word processing programs. Look for Copy and Paste commands in the Edit menu. (First copy the text with the Copy command; then paste the copy with the Paste command.)

7. Press **Enter**.

This step completes the copy. You now have two copies of the text: one in the original location and one in the new location.

REVIEW

1. Select the text you want to copy.

2. Press **Ctrl-F4** (Move).

3. Type **B** to select Block.

4. Type **C** to select Copy.

5. Move the cursor to where you want the copy to appear.

6. Press **Enter**.

To copy text

Move text

Oops!
Follow this same procedure to move the text back to its original location.

before

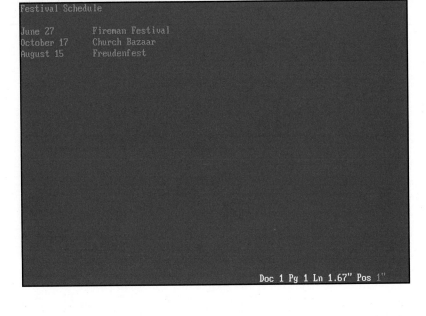

```
Festival Schedule

June 27         Fireman Festival
October 17      Church Bazaar
August 15       Freudenfest




                                    Doc 1 Pg 1 Ln 1.67" Pos 1"
```

1. **Type the text in the Before screen.**

   Use tabs to separate the date from the festival name. Be sure to press Enter after each line—including the last line.

2. **Use the arrow keys to move the cursor before the _A_ in _August_.**

   This step places the cursor at the start of the text you want to move.

3. **Select the entire line.**

   To select text, use the Block key combination—Alt-F4. See _TASK: Select text_ for help with this step.

4. **Press Ctrl-F4.**

   Ctrl-F4 is the Move key combination. You can move or copy text using this key combination. You see the prompt Move: 1 Block; 2 Tabular Column; 3 Rectangle: 0.

5. **Type B.**

   This step selects Block from the list of choices. You see the prompt 1 Move; 2 Copy; 3 Delete; 4 Append: 0.

6. **Type M.**

   This step selects Move from the list of choices.

Easy **PC**

Festival Schedule

June 27   Fireman Festival
August 15   Freudenfest
October 17   Church Bazaar

Doc 1 Pg 1 Ln 1.5" Pos 1"

after

Text runs together?
If you didn't insert a blank line or select the entire line, the two lines may run together. If so, position the cursor at the start of the second line and press Enter to separate the two lines.

7. Use the arrow keys to move the cursor under the *O* in *October*.

   This step places the cursor where you want the copied text to appear.

8. Press **Enter**.

   This step completes the move. The text appears in the new location, but not the original location.

Use a different program?
The Ctrl-F4 key combination does not work in other word processing programs. Look for Cut and Paste commands in the Edit menu. (First cut the text with the Cut command; then paste the text with the Paste command.)

REVIEW

To move text

1. Select the text that you want to move.

2. Press **Ctrl-F4** (Move).

3. Type **B** to select Block.

4. Type **M** to select Move.

5. Move the cursor to where you want the text to appear.

6. Press **Enter**.

Make text bold

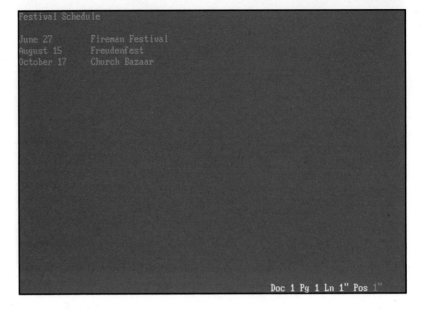

1. **Use the arrow keys to move the cursor before the *F* in *Festival*.**

   This step places the cursor at the start of the text that you want to change.

2. **Select the entire line.**

   To select text, use the Block key combination—Alt-F4. See *TASK: Select text* for help with this step.

3. **Press F6.**

   F6 is the Bold key. This step makes the selected text bold.

Festival Schedule

June 27   Fireman Festival
August 15   Freudenfest
October 17   Church Bazaar

Doc 1 Pg 1 Ln 1" Pos 2.7"

after

1. Select the text that you want to change.

2. Press **F6** (Bold).

To make text bold

Apply other formatting
For information on changing other text attributes (such as italics and underlining) in WordPerfect, see *Easy WordPerfect*.

Save a document

before

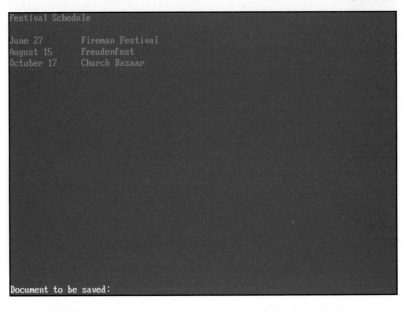

Oops!
If you do not want to save the document, press the F1 key after step 1; then exit the program without saving. See *TASK: Exit a word processing program.*

1. **Press F10.**

   F10 is the Save key. When you press it, you see the prompt `Document to be saved:.`

2. **Type FESTIVAL.WP5.**

   FESTIVAL.WP5 is the name that you want to assign the file. A file name consists of two parts: the file name and an optional extension. For the file name, you can type up to eight characters. The extension, which can be up to three characters long, usually indicates the type of file. A period separates the file name and the extension. As a general rule, use only letters and numbers for file names.

3. **Press Enter.**

   This step confirms the name and saves the document to disk. The document remains on-screen so that you can continue working. The file name you assigned appears in the lower left corner of the screen.

Easy PCs

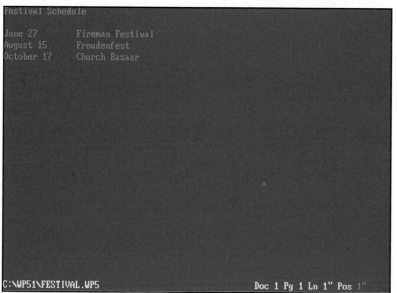

Festival Schedule

June 27   Fireman Festival
August 15   Freudenfest
October 17   Church Bazaar

C:\WP51\FESTIVAL.WP5   Doc 1 Pg 1 Ln 1" Pos 1"

after

Use other methods
You can save a file in
many different ways. For
additional ways to save a
WordPerfect file, see
Easy WordPerfect or
Using WordPerfect 5.1,
Special Edition.

REVIEW

1. Press **F10** (Save).

2. Type a file name.

3. Press **Enter**.

To save a document

Use a different program?
The F10 key does not
work in other word
processing programs.
Look for a Save
command in the File
menu or see your
application manual.

Open a document

before

Doc 1 Pg 1 Ln 1" Pos 1"

Oops!
If you highlight a file name and then press Enter, the document is only displayed—not opened. Press the F7 key, and then type R to retrieve (or open) the document.

1. **Start from a blank screen.**

   If you have a document on-screen, first save the document. See *TASK: Save a document*. Then press the F7 key (Exit) and type N twice. This step clears the document. For more information on clearing a document in WordPerfect, see *Easy WordPerfect* or *Using WordPerfect 5.1*, Special Edition.

2. **Press F5.**

   F5 is the List key. You use this key to work on files—retrieve, delete, copy, move, and so on. You see the name of the current directory at the bottom of the screen.

3. **Press Enter.**

   Pressing Enter tells WordPerfect to display files in the current directory. The List Files screen appears. This screen lists file names and includes the prompt 1 Retrieve; 2 Delete; 3 Move/Rename; 4 Print; 5 Short/Long Display; 6 Look; 7 Other Directory; 8 Copy; 9 Find; N Name Search: 6.

4. **Press the ↓ key until you highlight the file FESTIVAL.WP5.**

   This step moves the highlight bar to the file you want to open. If you do not have this file, select one that you do have.

5. **Type R.**

   Typing R selects Retrieve from the list of choices. The document you selected appears on-screen.

Easy **PCs**

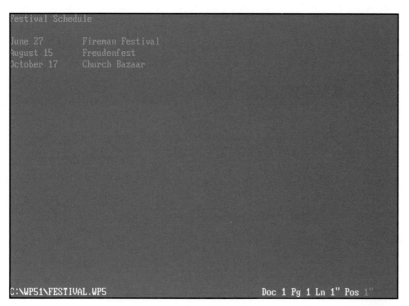

Festival Schedule

June 27   Fireman Festival
August 15   Freudenfest
October 17   Church Bazaar

C:\WP51\FESTIVAL.WP5   Doc 1 Pg 1 Ln 1" Pos 1"

after

1. Clear the screen.

2. Press **F5** (List).

3. Press **Enter**.

4. Use the arrow keys to highlight the file you want to open.

5. Type **R** to retrieve the file.

To open a document

Use a different program?
The F5 key does not work in other word processing programs. Look for an Open or Retrieve command in the File menu. Or see your application manual.

Using a Spreadsheet Program

(Excel)

This section includes the following tasks:

Start a spreadsheet program

Exit a spreadsheet program

Get help

Enter text

Enter a number

Create a formula

Edit a cell

Erase a cell

Undo a change

Copy a cell

Move a cell

Save a worksheet

Open a worksheet

Start a spread-sheet program

before

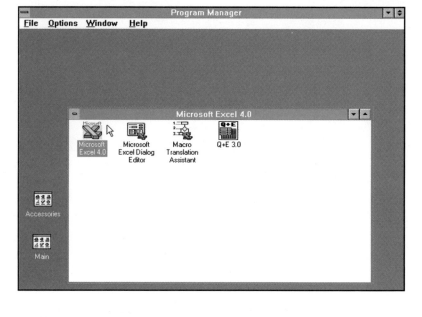

Oops!
Be sure to double-click the mouse button. If nothing happens, you may have waited too long between clicks. Try double-clicking again.

1. **Turn on the computer and monitor.**

   For help with this task, see *TASK: Turn on the computer*. You should see the DOS prompt (C:\>) on-screen. To start the program, you have to first start Microsoft Windows.

2. **Type win and press Enter.**

   Win is the command to start Microsoft Windows. You see the Program Manager on-screen. The Program Manager is an application that comes with Microsoft Windows.

   You must open Microsoft Windows before you can use Excel. Other spreadsheet programs, such as Lotus 1-2-3 and Quattro Pro, may not require this step. For more information on Microsoft Windows, see the section Working with Microsoft Windows earlier in the Task/Review part of this book.

3. **Double-click on the group icon for Microsoft Excel.**

   To double-click, click the mouse button twice in rapid succession. This step opens the Excel window. The Before screen shows the Excel window.

   In Microsoft Windows programs, the easiest way to use the program is to use a mouse. See the Basics part for more information on how to use a mouse.

4. **Double-click on the program icon for Microsoft Excel.**

   This step starts the Excel program. You see a blank worksheet on-screen.

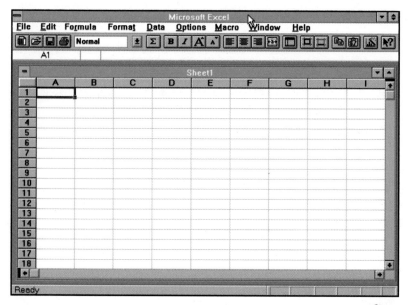

after

Use a different program?
If you use Lotus 1-2-3 or Quattro Pro for DOS, you start the program from the DOS prompt. See *TASK: Start a DOS program*. If you use Lotus 1-2-3 for Windows or Quattro Pro for Windows, follow the procedure described here, although you will click on the icon for that program—not the Microsoft Excel icon.

1. Turn on your computer and monitor.

2. Type win and press Enter.

3. Double-click on the group icon for Microsoft Excel.

4. Double-click on the program icon for Microsoft Excel.

To start a spread-sheet program

Exit Excel
To exit Excel, see *TASK: Exit a spreadsheet*

Exit a spread-sheet program

before

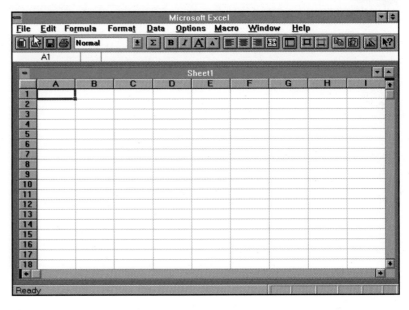

Oops!
To restart Excel,
see *TASK: Start a
spreadsheet program.*

1. **Click on File in the menu bar.**

   This step opens the File menu. You see a list of File commands.

2. **Click on Exit.**

   This step chooses the Exit command. You return to the Microsoft Windows Program Manager. The After screen shows this step.

   To exit Microsoft Windows and return to DOS, follow steps 3 through 5.

3. **In the Program Manager, click on File in the menu bar.**

   This step opens the File menu.

4. **Click on Exit Windows.**

   This step selects the Exit Windows command. On-screen you see the Exit Windows dialog box.

5. **Point to OK and click the left mouse button.**

   This step confirms that you do want to exit. You return to DOS. You see the prompt C:\> on-screen.

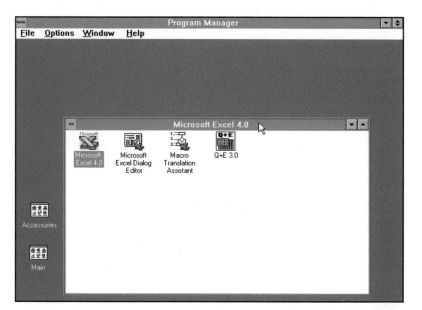

after

Exit other programs
Use this procedure to exit
most Microsoft Windows
programs. For information
on exiting DOS programs,
see *TASK: Exit a DOS
program.*

REVIEW

1. Click on **File** in the menu bar.

2. Click on the **Exit** command.

   To exit Microsoft Windows, follow steps 3 through 5.

3. Click on **File** in the menu bar.

4. Click on the **Exit Windows** command.

5. Click on **OK**.

To exit a spread-sheet program

Get help

before

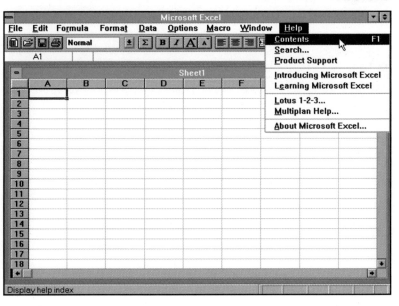

Oops!
To close the Help window
quickly, double-click on
the Control menu box.
This box is the small bar
to the left of the
window's title bar.

1. Click on **Help** in the menu bar.

   This step opens the Help menu. On-screen you see a list of Help commands.

2. Click on **Contents**.

   This step chooses the Contents command. The Help window opens, and you see a list of topics.

3. Click on **Worksheets**.

   This step selects a topic. When the mouse pointer is on a topic for which you can get help, the pointer changes to a hand with a pointing finger. You see a list of subtopics.

4. Click on **Creating a new worksheet**.

   This step chooses the topic and displays the steps you follow to create a new worksheet.

5. In the Help menu bar, click on **File**.

   This step opens the File menu. Be sure to click on the File menu within the Help window.

6. Click on **Exit**.

   This step selects the Exit command and closes the Help window.

Easy **PCs**

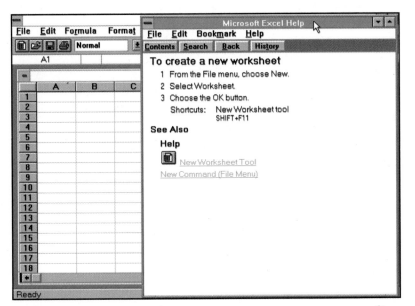

after

REVIEW

1. Click on **Help** in the menu bar.

2. Click on the **Contents** command.

3. Click on the topic for which you want help.

4. Click on the subtopic for which you want help.

5. To close Help, click on **File** in the Help menu bar.

6. Click on the **Exit** command.

To get help

Use a different program?
This procedure should work for most Microsoft Windows programs. To get help in a DOS spreadsheet (or other) program, try pressing the F1 key. Or check your application manual for instructions.

TASK

Enter text

before

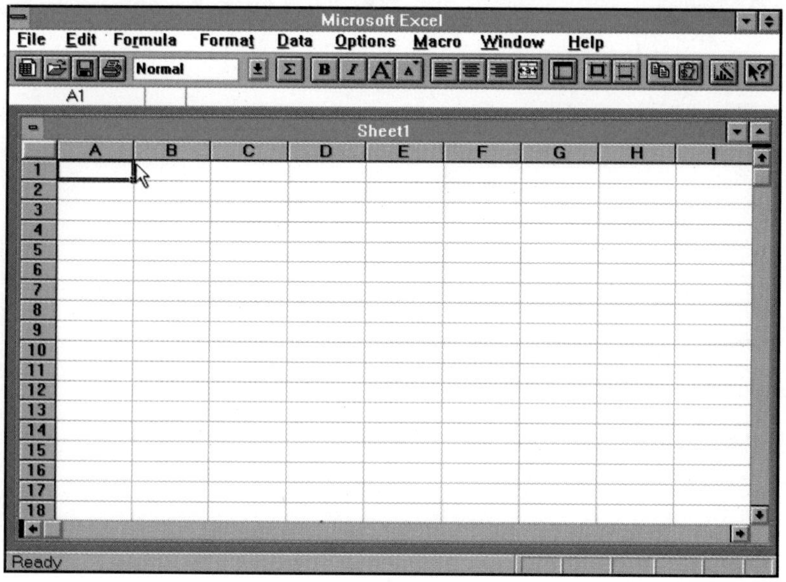

Microsoft Excel — Sheet1 (spreadsheet screenshot)

Oops!
To delete the most recent text entry, select the Edit Undo Entry command.

1. **Select cell A1.**

   This step makes A1 the active cell. In Excel, the active cell on a worksheet appears with a bold border. If you are using a mouse, click on cell A1. If you are using the keyboard, use the arrow keys to move to this cell.

   Each cell in a spreadsheet has a unique name. A cell name is formed by combining the column and row locations into one description. For example, A1 describes the intersection of column A and row 1.

2. **Type Sales Results.**

   This step enters the title of your worksheet. The text appears on-screen in the formula bar—an area under the menu bar. Other spreadsheet programs have a similar area where the entry is displayed, but it is often called something different, such as the control panel.

3. **Press Enter.**

   Pressing Enter accepts the entry in the formula bar and enters it into the cell.

166

Easy **PCs**

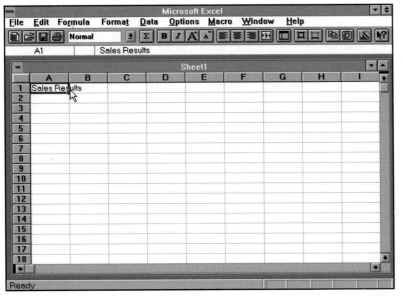

after

Use another program?
Follow this same
procedure to enter text in
other spreadsheet
programs. All programs
use a cell reference (row
number and column
letter). You can usually
use a mouse or the arrow
keys to select a cell.

1. Select the cell in which you want to enter text.

2. Type the text.

3. Press **Enter** or any arrow key.

To enter text

Make a mistake?
If you make a mistake
when typing the entry,
use Backspace to correct
the entry. The entry is not
placed in the cell until you
press Enter or an arrow
key.

Enter a number

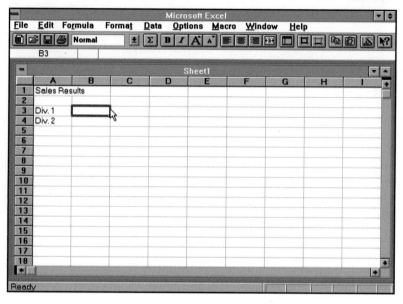

Oops!
To delete a text entry, select Edit Undo Entry immediately after typing the entry.

1. **Select cell B3.**

   This step makes B3 the active cell. If you are using a mouse, click on cell B3. If you are using the keyboard, use the arrow keys to move to this cell.

2. **Type 4250.**

   The value—4250—appears in the formula bar. If you make a mistake, use the Backspace key to correct the entry. (The Backspace key erases the character to the left of the cursor.) The entry is not placed in the cell until you press Enter or an arrow key.

3. **Press the ↓ key.**

   Pressing the ↓ key accepts the entry, enters the value into the cell, and makes B4 the active cell.

   Note that the entry is right-aligned and that no decimal places, commas, or dollar signs are displayed—this is the default format for numbers. You can change this format. See *Easy Excel* or *Using Excel 4 for Windows*, Special Edition.

Easy **PCs**

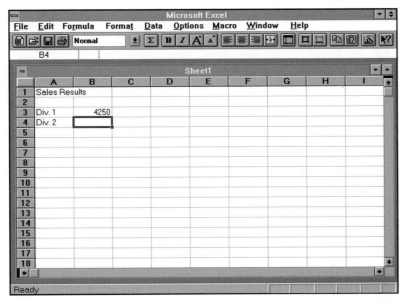

after

Enter a negative number
To enter a negative number, type a minus sign, and then type the number.

1. Select the cell in which you want to enter the number.

2. Type the number.

3. Press **Enter** or any arrow key.

To enter a number

Use a different program?
This same procedure works for all spreadsheet programs.

Using a Spreadsheet Program

Create a formula

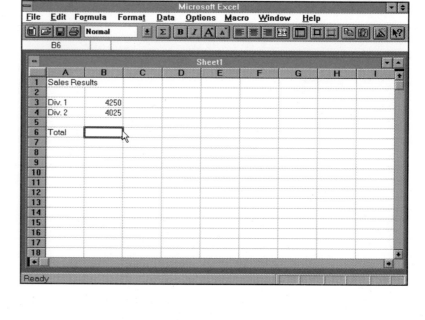

Oops!
To delete the entry, select Edit Undo Entry immediately after typing it.

1. **Select cell B6.**

   This step makes B6 the active cell; the answer to the formula will appear in this cell. If you are using a mouse, click on cell B6. If you are using the keyboard, use the arrow keys to move to this cell.

   Remember to type the information in the Before screen before you begin this task.

2. **Type =.**

   Typing = tells Excel that you want to enter a formula. To add the contents of two or more cells, you create an addition formula. You can create any type of formula—addition, subtraction, multiplication, and so on.

3. **Select cell B3.**

   B3 is the first cell that you want to include in the addition formula. If you are using a mouse, point to cell B3 and click the left mouse button. If you are using the keyboard, use the arrow keys to move to this cell. The cell is surrounded by a dashed box, called a *marquee*. You see =B3 in the formula bar and in cell B6.

4. **Press +.**

   The + sign is the operator. It tells Excel which mathematical operation you want to perform—in this case, addition. B6 again becomes the active cell.

5. **Select cell B4.**

   Cell B4 is the second cell that you want to include in the formula. You can select this cell by using the mouse or use the arrow keys.

Easy PCs

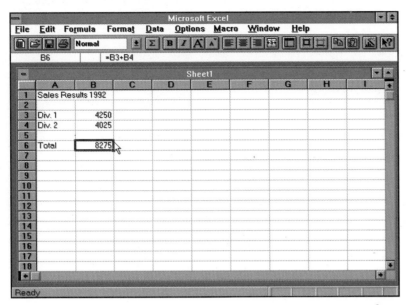

after

A dashed marquee surrounds the cell. Notice that both the formula bar and cell B6 contain the formula =B3+B4.

6. **Press Enter.**

Pressing Enter tells Excel that you are finished with the addition formula. You see the results of the formula in cell B6. The formula bar displays the actual formula (=B3+B4)—not the result.

You can include any cells in your formula; the cells do not have to be next to each other. Also, you can use different operations and combine mathematical operations—for instance, C3+C4–D5.

1. Select the cell in which you want to enter the formula.

2. Type =.

3. Select the first cell that you want to include in the formula.

4. Type the operator (such as + or –).

5. Select the second cell that you want to include in the formula.

6. Continue typing the operator and selecting cells until the formula includes all the cells you want.

7. Press **Enter**.

What are the benefits of a formula?
You could have just typed the values in the formula, but then if you change the cell contents, the formula would be incorrect. Because a formula references the cell that contains the value, the formula changes when the value changes.

To create a formula

Use a different program?
If you use Lotus 1-2-3 or Quattro Pro, the steps you follow are the same, except that you type + for step 2 and you do not see a dashed marquee around the active cell.

Edit a cell

before

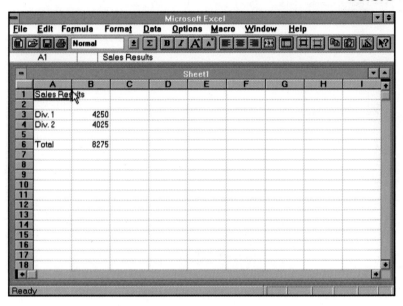

Oops!
To undo the edit, select the Edit Undo Entry command immediately after you edit the text.

1. **Select cell A1.**

   This step makes A1 the active cell. If you are using a mouse, click on cell A1. If you are using the keyboard, use the arrow keys to move to this cell. This cell contains the entry that you want to change.

2. **Press F2.**

   F2 is the Edit key. Pressing this key moves the cursor to the formula bar. The cursor is at the end of the entry. An X and a check mark appear before the entry. (Clicking on the X cancels the change; clicking on the check mark confirms the new entry.)

   You can use the arrow keys to move the cursor to the characters that you want to change or delete. You also can press the Backspace key to delete characters.

3. **Press the space bar once.**

   This step inserts a space between the original text and the text you are about to type.

4. **Type 1992.**

   This step changes the worksheet title from *Sales Results* to *Sales Results 1992*.

5. **Press Enter.**

   Pressing Enter accepts the new entry.

Easy **PCs**

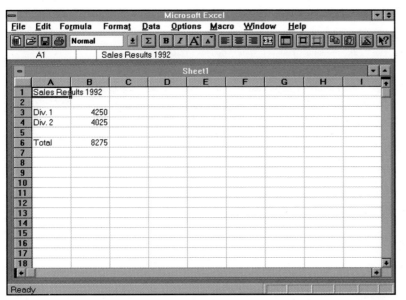

after

Change your mind?
Before you press Enter to accept the entry, you can press the Esc key to cancel the changes.

1. Select the cell that you want to edit.

2. Press **F2** (Edit).

3. Edit the entry.

4. Press **Enter**.

To edit a cell

Use a different program?
This procedure also works in Lotus 1-2-3 and Quattro Pro.

Erase a cell

Oops!
To undo the most recent deletion, select the Edit Undo Clear command.

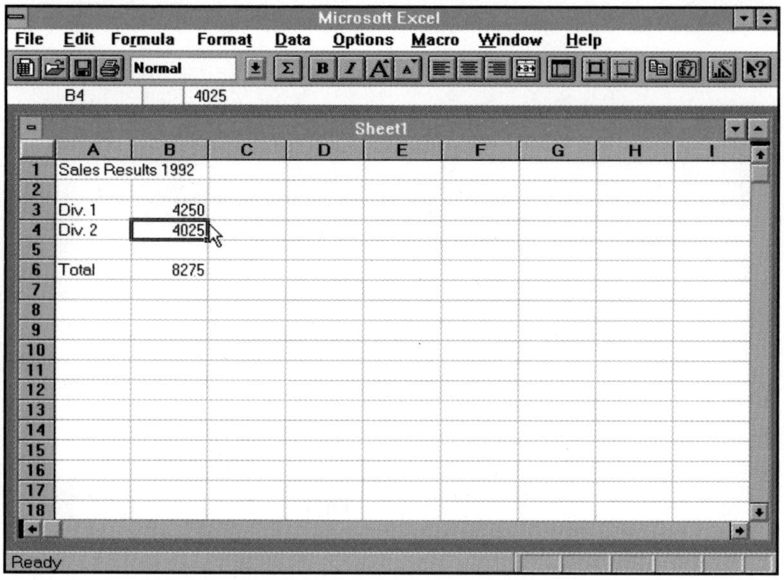

1. **Select cell B4.**

   This step makes B4 the active cell; B4 is the cell that you want to erase. If you are using a mouse, click on cell B4. If you are using the keyboard, use the arrow keys to move to this cell. You see the current entry—4025—in the formula bar.

2. **Press Del.**

   Pressing the Del key displays the Clear dialog box. You can select to clear All, Formats, Formulas, or Notes. (For a complete discussion of these options, see *Using Excel 4 for Windows*, Special Edition.) The default, Formulas, is selected.

3. **Click on OK.**

   This step deletes the entry in the cell, but retains the cell's formatting. If the cell is included in any formulas, the formulas are updated automatically.

Easy **PCs**

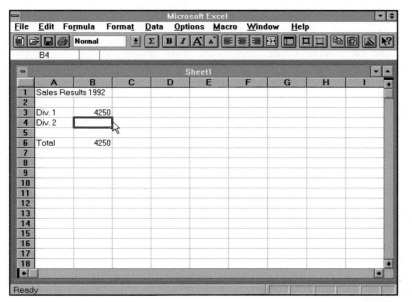

after

Use a different program?
In Lotus 1-2-3 and Quattro Pro, the Clear dialog box section does not appear. Pressing Del (step 2 of the Task section) completes the task.

1. Select the cell that you want to erase.

2. Press **Del**.

3. Click on **OK**.

To erase a cell

Undo a change

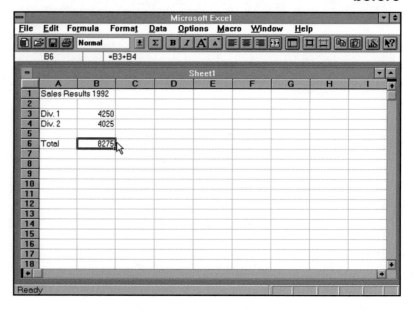

Oops!
Select the Edit Redo command to undo the "undo."

1. **Select cell B6.**

   This step makes cell B6 the active cell. If you are using a mouse, click on cell B6. If you are using the keyboard, use the arrow keys to move to this cell. You see the current entry in the formula bar—=B3+B4. Notice that this entry is a formula.

2. **Type 2000 and press Enter.**

   This step overwrites the formula with the number 2000. When you edit the worksheet, you want to be sure not to overwrite formulas. If you do, the figures may not be correct if the formula has been deleted. Therefore, you want to undo this change.

3. **Click on Edit in the menu bar.**

   This step opens the Edit menu.

4. **Click on Undo Entry.**

   This step selects the Undo command. The cell is returned to its original form. Note that the Before and After figures are identical because the worksheet is returned to its original form.

   Depending on the action you have taken in Excel, the name of the Undo command will change. (For instance, it may be called Undo Entry, Undo Paste, and so on.) If the command is not available, it will be called Can't Undo and will appear gray.

   You must select the Edit Undo command immediately after completing the action that you want to undo. Undo always undoes the last operation. Also, you can only undo certain tasks. Basically, you can undo any changes made to worksheet entries—deleting,

176

Easy **PCs**

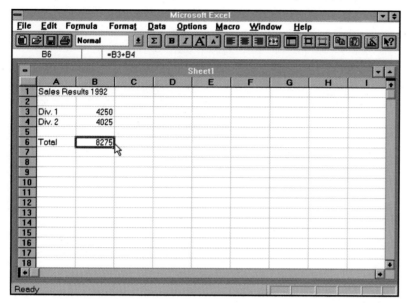

after

moving, copying, and so on. You cannot undo command settings, format settings, and style commands. See your Excel manual or *Using Excel 4 for Windows,* Special Edition, for more information.

Use a different program?
In Lotus 1-2-3, press the Alt-F4 key combination to undo a change. In Quattro Pro, press the Alt-F5 key combination. See *Easy 1-2-3* or *Easy Quattro Pro* for more information.

REVIEW

1. Click on **Edit** in the menu bar.

2. Click on the **Undo** command.

To undo a change

Copy a cell

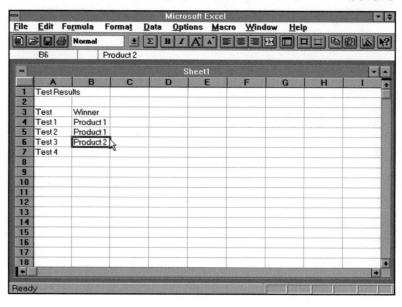

Oops!
To undo the most recent copy, select the Edit Undo Paste command and press the Esc key.

1. **Select cell B6.**

   This step makes cell B6 the active cell; this is the cell whose contents you want to copy. If you are using a mouse, click on cell B6. If you are using the keyboard, use the arrow keys to move to this cell.

2. **Click on Edit in the menu bar.**

   This step opens the Edit menu.

3. **Click on Copy.**

   This step selects the Copy command. Next you need to tell Excel where to put the copy.

4. **Select cell B7.**

   This step makes B7 the active cell. You want the copy to appear in this cell. Use the mouse or the arrow keys to select cell B7.

5. **Press Enter.**

   Pressing Enter confirms the copy. The entry appears in both cells— B6 and B7. Note that Excel copies both the entry and the format (alignment, protection settings, and so on).

Easy **PCs**

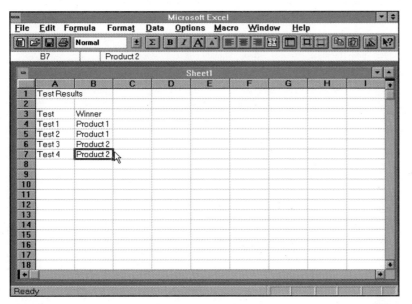

after

Use a different program?
To copy a cell in Lotus 1-2-3, use the Copy command. To copy a cell in Quattro Pro, use the Edit Copy command. Remember that you access the menu bar by pressing the slash (/) key in these programs.

REVIEW

1. Select the cell that you want to copy.

2. Click on **Edit** in the menu bar.

3. Click on the **Copy** command.

4. Select the cell in which you want the copy to appear.

5. Press **Enter**.

To copy a cell

Move a cell

```
─                        Microsoft Excel                    ▼ ▲
File  Edit  Formula  Format  Data  Options  Macro  Window  Help
┌──┬──┬──┐ ┌────────┐ ┌──┐┌──┐┌──┐┌──┐┌──┐┌──┐┌──┐┌──┐┌──┐┌──┐┌──┐
│  │  │  │ │ Normal │ │±││Σ││B││I││A`││A`││≣││≣││≣││⊞││□││⊡││⊟││🗐││🗎││🖾││N?│
└──┴──┴──┘ └────────┘ └──┘└──┘└──┘└──┘└──┘└──┘└──┘└──┘└──┘└──┘└──┘
     D5              │  86
─                          Sheet1                          ▼ ▲
     A       B       C      D      E      F      G      H      I
 1  Test Results
 2
 3  Test    Winner  Score
 4  Test 1  Product 1       88
 5  Test 2  Product 1              86
 6  Test 3  Product 2
 7  Test 4  Product 2
 8
 9
10
11
12
13
14
15
16
17
18
Ready
```

Oops!
To undo the most recent move, select Edit Undo Paste, and then press the Esc key.

1. **Select cell D5.**

   This step makes D5 the active cell; D5 is the cell that you want to move. If you are using a mouse, click on cell D5. If you are using the keyboard, use the arrow keys to move to this cell.

2. **Click on Edit in the menu bar.**

   This step opens the Edit menu. You see a list of Edit commands.

3. **Click on Cut.**

   This step selects the Cut command.

4. **Select cell C5.**

   This step makes cell C5 the active cell. This cell is where you want the entry to appear. Use the mouse or arrow keys to select cell C5.

5. **Press Enter.**

   Pressing Enter confirms the move. The entry is cut from the original location and pasted to the new location.

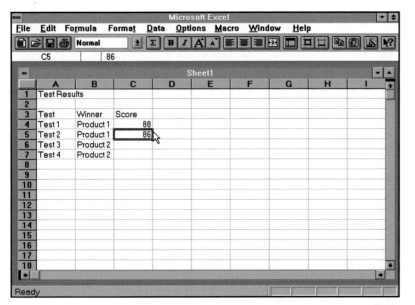

after

Use a different program?
In Lotus 1-2-3, use the Move command. In Quattro Pro, use the Edit Move command. Remember that you access the menu bar by pressing the slash (/) key in these programs.

1. Select the cell that you want to move.

2. Click on **Edit** in the menu bar.

3. Click on the **Cut** command.

4. Select the cell in which you want the entry to appear.

5. Press **Enter**.

To move a cell

Save a worksheet

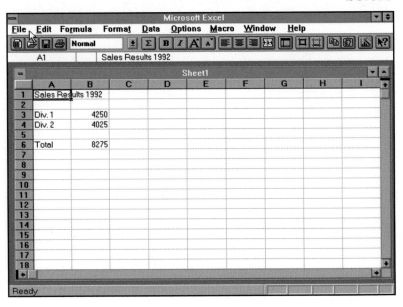

1. Click on **File** in the menu bar.

   This step opens the File menu. You see a list of File commands.

2. Click on **Save**.

   This step selects the Save command. The first time you save the worksheet, you see the Save As dialog box. The cursor is positioned in the File Name text box.

3. Type **SALES92**.

   This step assigns the name SALES92 to the file. The file name can be up to eight characters long. As a general rule, use only alphanumeric characters. You do not need to type an extension. Excel automatically adds the XLS extension.

4. Click on **OK**.

   You are returned to the worksheet. In the title bar, you see the file name, SALES92.XLS.

Easy **PCs**

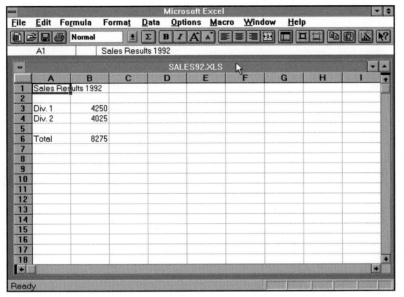

after

REVIEW

Save often
Until you save the worksheet, the data you have created is not committed to disk. You can lose the data if something happens, such as a power loss. As you work on the worksheet, the changes you make are not updated on disk until you save the file Be sure to save the worksheet periodically.

1. Click on **File** in the menu bar.

2. Click on the **Save** command.

3. Type the file name.

4. Click on **OK**.

To save a worksheet

Use a different program?
To save a worksheet in Lotus 1-2-3 or Quattro Pro, use the File Save command. Remember that you access the menu bar by pressing the slash (/) key in these programs.

Open a worksheet

before

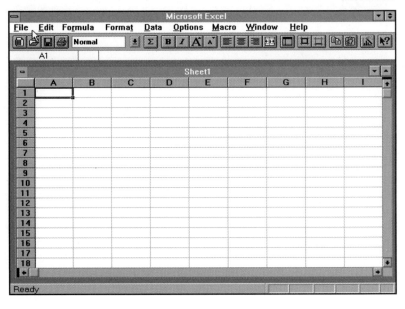

Oops!
If you open the wrong worksheet, use the File Close command to close the worksheet. Then try again.

1. **Click on File in the menu bar.**

   This step opens the File menu. You see a list of File commands.

2. **Click on Open.**

   This step selects the Open command. You see the Open dialog box. The cursor is positioned in the File Name text box.

3. **Type SALES92.**

   SALES92 is the name of the file that you want to open. You can type the file name, if you know it, or you can use the mouse or arrow keys to select the file name from the Files list. You do not have to type the extension.

4. **Click on OK.**

   This step confirms that you want to open the worksheet. The worksheet is opened and appears on-screen. The file name appears in the title bar.

Easy **PCs**

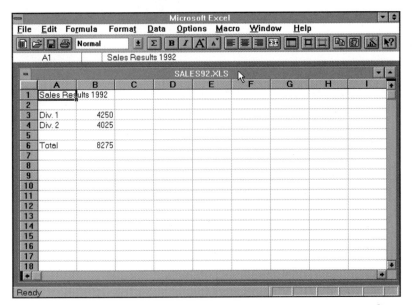

after

Use a different program?
To save a worksheet in Lotus 1-2-3 or Quattro Pro, use the File Retrieve command. Remember that you access the menu bar by pressing the slash (/) key in these programs.

To open a worksheet

1. Click on **File** in the menu bar.

2. Click on the **Open** command.

3. Type or point to the file name.

4. Click on the **OK** button.

Reference

Software Guide

Troubleshooting Guide

DOs and DON'Ts

Questions and Answers

Glossary

Easy **PCs**

Software Guide

To use your computer to perform specific tasks (such as writing a letter, balancing a budget, storing real estate clients), you need to purchase and install applications. *Applications* are tools you use on the computer.

This guide discusses the most common categories of applications, briefly explains what each type does, and lists a few representative software packages. For more information, see Que's *Introduction to PCs,* 2nd Edition, or pick up any personal computing magazine (such as *PC World*, *PCWeek*, or *PC Magazine*) and read the ads. Que also publishes books on the more popular software packages, such as Microsoft Windows, WordPerfect, and Lotus 1-2-3.

Types of Applications

There are basically 11 categories of applications:

- Word processors
- Spreadsheets
- Databases
- Graphics
- Desktop publishing
- Integrated programs
- Financial
- Utility
- Communication
- Education
- Games

The following sections discuss each type.

A Word About Microsoft Windows

Some programs are designed specifically to work with Microsoft Windows. These programs work essentially in the same way. After you learn one Microsoft Windows program, you can easily learn other Microsoft Windows programs.

The most popular programs are available in both DOS and Microsoft Windows versions. Microsoft Windows programs are noted in the following sections. To use these programs, you must have Microsoft Windows.

Word Processors

You use *word processors* to create memos, letters, reports, brochures, and other printed material. A word processor is like a typewriter—but much better.

Most word processors offer several features that make it easy to work with text. With a word processor, you can complete these tasks:

See text as you type on-screen. Because the text is not committed to paper, you can make changes and corrections—delete text, add text, and so on.

Rearrange text. As you write, you may decide that the last paragraph really belongs in the introduction. With a word processor, you can move the text from one spot to another. This process is called *cut and paste*.

Check the spelling in your document. Nothing mars a document worse than a glaring typo or misspelled word. Most word processors offer a spelling checker that lets you check a document for typos before you print it.

Save the document. You can save the document on disk and use it again.

Format the document. Word processors vary in the formatting features they offer. Simple word processors enable you to set tabs, change margins, and select different fonts or font styles (bold, italic, and so on). Complex word processors include these features, but they also enable you to add headers and footers, create columns, insert graphics, and so on.

These are the most common word processing programs:

- Ami Pro (Windows)
- Microsoft Word for DOS
- Microsoft Word for Windows
- WordPerfect
- WordPerfect for Windows
- WordStar

The following is a screen for the DOS version of WordPerfect:

The following is a screen for Word for Windows:

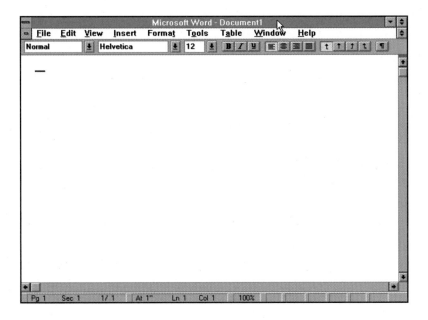

Spreadsheets

A *spreadsheet* is an electronic version of an accountant's pad. You use a spreadsheet program to set up worksheets. *Worksheets* can total sales by division, keep track of a monthly budget, figure loan balances, and perform other financial analysis.

With a spreadsheet program, you can complete these tasks:

Calculate formulas. You can write formulas—from simple to complex—to add, subtract, multiply, and divide. You can depend on the spreadsheet program to calculate the results correctly every time.

Change data and recalculate. You can change, add, or delete data, and recalculate the results automatically. You no longer have to erase and rewrite when you forget a crucial figure. And you don't have to manually refigure all the amounts when you do make a change or an addition.

Rearrange data. With your worksheet on-screen, you can add or delete a column or row. You can copy and move data from one spot to another.

Repeat information. You can copy text, a value, or a formula to another place in the worksheet. For instance, in your monthly budget worksheet you total the expenses for each month. You can, for example, write a formula that calculates January's totals, and then copy this formula for February through December.

Change the format of data. You can format your results in many ways. You can display a number with dollar signs, as a percent, or as a date. You can align text left, right, or center.

Print data. You can print reports of your data.

Create charts. Most spreadsheet programs enable you to graph your data and print that graph. You can create pie graphs, bar graphs, and line graphs, as well as many other graph types.

These are the most common spreadsheet programs:

- 1-2-3
- 1-2-3 for Windows
- Microsoft Excel (Windows)
- Quattro Pro
- Quattro Pro for Windows

The following is a screen from the DOS version of 1-2-3:

The following is a screen from Excel for Windows:

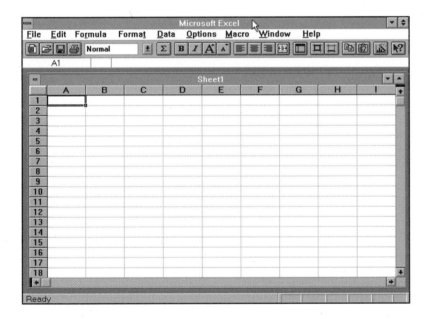

Databases

A *database* is similar to a complex card file. You store
related information together. For instance, you can use a

database to keep track of real estate clients, a baseball card collection, employees, inventory—any set of data.

Each piece of data is stored in a *field*—for instance, a phone number. A set of fields make up a *record*—for instance, a name, address, and phone number. A *database* is a collection of all the records.

With a database, you can complete these tasks:

Retrieve data. After you enter data, you can easily retrieve it. Suppose, for example, that you are looking for a specific invoice. You no longer need to sift through several paper documents; instead, you can quickly pull the invoice up on-screen.

Sort data. You can rearrange data. For instance, you may want an alphabetical list of clients sorted by last name to use as a phone list. You may want to sort the same list by zip code to do a mailing. A database lets you arrange the same address list in several different ways.

Print data. You can print reports, mailing labels, and other documents.

These are some of the most common database packages:

- dBASE
- FoxPro
- Paradox
- Paradox for Windows
- Personal R:Base
- Q&A

The following is a screen from Q&A:

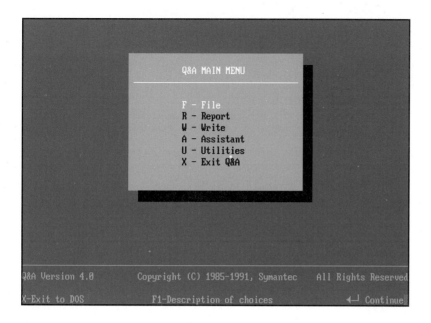

Graphics

With graphics programs, you can create illustrations: from simple line art to complex drawings. Also included in this category are presentation programs that enable you to create graphs and computer-aided design (CAD) programs that let you create architectural and other complex drawings.

With graphics programs, you can do the following:

Use many drawing tools. The tools offered by packages vary. You can draw geometric shapes (circles, squares, rectangles, and lines), add fills and color, create text, trace objects, align objects, and so on.

Edit drawings. If you don't get the drawing just right, you can modify it. You can delete parts of the drawing and redraw them.

Create drawings to be used over and over. You might, for instance, create a logo that you can use on hundreds of company documents.

These are some graphics programs:

- AutoCAD (CAD)
- CorelDRAW! (draw)
- Generic CADD (CAD)
- Harvard Graphics (charts)
- Harvard Graphics for Windows (charts)
- PC Paintbrush (draw—Windows)
- PowerPoint (charts—Windows)

The following is a screen from PC Paintbrush:

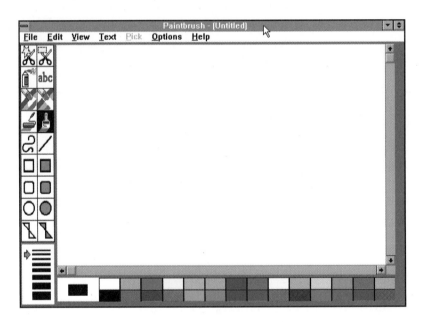

The following is a screen from Harvard Graphics:

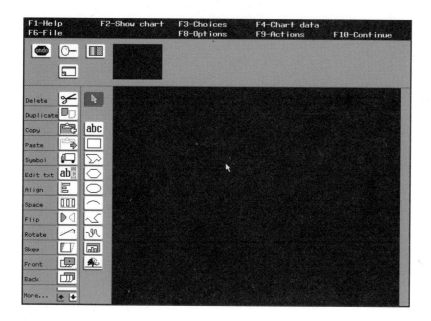

Desktop Publishing

Desktop publishing programs enable you to create sophisticated brochures, newsletters, fliers, resumes, menus, reports, and other output. Some word processing packages offer desktop publishing capabilities (such as column layout), but the features offered by desktop publishing programs are more sophisticated. Keep in mind that if you do use a desktop publishing program, you will probably also need to use a word processor to create the text.

With a desktop publishing program, you can complete the following tasks:

Lay out a page. With a desktop publishing program, you have precise control over the layout of the page—the margins, headers, footers, and so on. You also have control over the text—what font, size, and style are used, where the text is placed, and how the text flows.

Change page layout. If you don't like how the document looks, you can experiment with the layout until you get the document just the way you want it.

Create templates. You can create a template for a document that you will use over and over—for instance, a newsletter. The headings and layout are set; you then just have to add the text.

These are the most popular desktop publishing packages:

- Microsoft Publisher (Windows)
- PageMaker (Windows)
- PFS: First Publisher
- Ventura Publisher (DOS and Windows)

The following is a screen from Ventura Publisher:

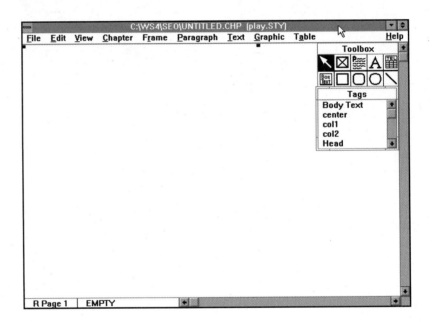

Integrated Programs

Integrated programs combine several types of programs into one package: word processing, database, spreadsheet, and communications. Each of these programs offer the benefits previously discussed. They also have the added benefit of allowing you to integrate the data from one program into the next. For instance, you can use the mailing list from your database to create form letters with your word processor. You can copy financial figures from the spreadsheet to a report in the word processor. On the down side, each of the programs will not offer as many features as "stand-alone" or dedicated packages.

Here are some examples of integrated programs:

- LotusWorks
- Microsoft Works (Windows)
- PFS: WindowWorks (Windows)
- PFS:First Choice

The following is a screen from PFS: WindowWorks:

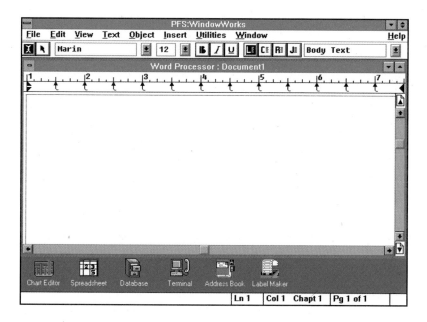

Financial Programs

Financial programs enable you to create tax returns, balance your checkbook, set up an accounting system, and perform other finance-related tasks. These programs range from the simple to the complex. Some examples follow:

- Microsoft Money (Windows check-writing program)

- Peachtree (complete accounting package—general ledger, accounts receivable, accounts payable, payroll)

- Quicken (simple check-writing program; also can be used for limited accounting purposes)

- TurboTax (tax preparation program)

The following is a screen from TurboTax:

The following is a screen from Quicken:

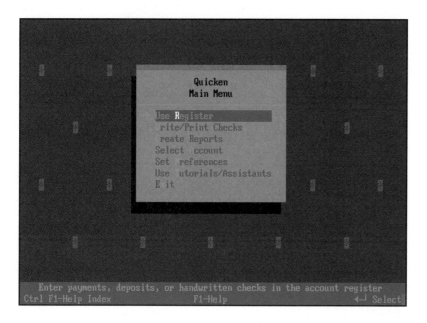

Utilities

Utility programs help you better manage your hardware and software. Different utility packages have different features. Here are some features you may find:

Faster and easier backups. Some utility packages provide a faster backup routine. Rather than type cryptic commands at the DOS prompt, you can perform a backup from a menu. You also have more control over the backup, such as specifying which files are backed up.

Undeleting files. Some utility packages enable you to recover lost files. They also may enable you to recover a formatted disk.

Recovering damaged files and disks. If you are an experienced user, you can use utility programs to help recover damaged files or disks.

Reference

201

Fine-tune the hard disk. Some utility programs enable you to increase the speed of your hard disk. (This process is called *optimizing*.) You also may be able to rearrange the files on your disk so that they require less space. (This process is called *defragmenting*.)

Here are some popular utility programs:

- The Norton Utilities
- PC Tools

The following is a screen from The Norton Utilities:

Communication

Communication programs enable you to use your computer to talk to other computers. You might, for example, need to access a huge computer (called a *mainframe*) that stores stock figures so that you can get up-to-the-minute reports. Or you might need some sales data from your district office's computer. With a communication program, you can send and receive information over the phone lines.

To use your computer to communicate, you must have a modem and a phone line. (For more information on modems, see *Introduction to Personal Computers*, 2nd Edition, or *Introduction to PC Communications*, published by Que.) And you need a communication package. PROCOMM PLUS is an example of this type of package.

Education

The computer is easy to use, which makes it ideal for learning new tasks. You can use programs to learn how to type, master a foreign language, plan a travel route for a trip, and accomplish many other educational tasks.

Games

And last but not least, you can use the computer to play games. Games can range from diagnosing and performing surgery on a patient (Life and Death) to playing golf (Mean 18 Ultimate Golf) to flying a plane (Flight Simulator).

The following is a screen from Solitaire:

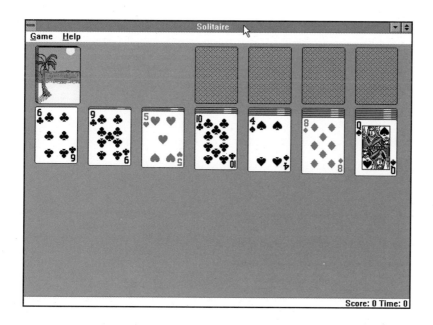

Others

Not all programs fit into a neat category. New programs are created every day. Programs are available that enable you to draw up a will, create a calendar, perform complex statistical analysis, and count calories. Just browse through some computer magazines (*PC World* or *PC Week*, for example) to get an idea of the world of possibilities. Explore with your computer. Be productive. But most of all, have fun.

Troubleshooting Guide

This guide provides some general troubleshooting advice. In particular, this guide covers problems you may encounter when starting the computer, finding files, using applications, and printing. This guide also covers how to prevent problems (or at least, how to be prepared for them).

Startup Problems

If you turn on your computer and nothing happens, do the following:

- Check to be sure that you have turned on everything. Is the system unit on? Is the monitor on? Is the power-strip on?

- Check to be sure that everything is plugged in. Is the system unit plugged in? Is the monitor plugged in? If you have one, is the powerstrip plugged in?

- Check all cables. Is the monitor cable connected to the system unit? Is the keyboard cable connected to the system unit?

- Check the brightness controls on the monitor. Have these controls been tinkered with so that you cannot see what is being displayed?

- Try turning on the computer again. Turn off the computer, wait a few minutes, and then turn it on again.

If you turn on the computer and get an error message, write down the error message. Check your computer manual or see *Using MS-DOS 5*.

If the error message says `Non-System disk or disk error`, check to see whether drive A (or B) contains a disk. If so, eject the disk and try starting the computer again.

File Problems

If you cannot find or access a file, do the following:

- Check your typing. Did you type the file name correctly? Are you sure that the name you typed is the exact name of the file?

- Check the directory. Remember that DOS can find files only in the current directory. Is the file in the current directory? If not, change directories and try again.

- Try the command again using wild-card characters. You may have thought you had given a file a certain name, but you might have made a mistake—even typing a single character differently can make a file hard to find. For instance, if you think you named the file CHAP01.DOC, type DIR *.DOC files to see all files with a DOC extension. You also can type CH*.* to see all files that have file names beginning with the characters CH. (For more information on wild cards, see *Easy DOS* or *Using MS-DOS 5*.)

- If the file is on a floppy disk, check to be sure that the disk is properly inserted into the floppy disk drive. If the file is on a 5 1/4-inch floppy disk, did you remember to shut the door of the disk drive after you inserted the disk?

Application Problems

If you encounter problems while working in an application program, do the following:

- If you get an error message, write it down. Sometimes you can get help on the error message by pressing the F1 key when the error message is displayed. You usually can clear the error message by pressing the Esc key. Check your application manual for help with the error message.

- If nothing seems to be happening (the computer is "hung"), listen and watch the lights on your computer. You may think that the computer isn't responding, but it may be busy loading a file or doing a calculation. If you hear the disks working or see the disk light flashing, wait.

- If you get an error message, display a dialog box or menu you don't want, or just generally get backed into a corner, try pressing the Esc key. If pressing the key once does nothing, try pressing it several times.

- If you are certain that the computer is "hung" (will not respond to anything you do) and nothing else works, press the Ctrl-Alt-Del key combination to reboot.

Printing Problems

If you have problems printing, do the following:

- Check to be sure that you have turned on everything. Is the system unit on? Is the printer on? Is the powerstrip on?

- Check to be sure that everything is plugged in. Is the system unit plugged in? Is the printer plugged in? If you have one, is the powerstrip plugged in?

- Check all cables. Is the printer cable connected to the system unit?

- Isolate the problem. Are the printer lights on? If so, the printer has power. Is the computer working? If so, the computer has power. If one or the other doesn't work, you have a clue to where the problem lies.

- Check that the printer has paper. If it doesn't, check your manual for help on how to load paper.

- Make sure that the right printer is selected from within the software package. (Check for a Printer Setup command in the File menu.) If you are using Microsoft Windows, use the Control Panel to set up the printer.

- Be sure that the printer has been set up properly. See your printer manual and application manual for help on setup.

Preventing Problems

Problems are inevitable; you cannot always avoid them, but you can be prepared for them. Here are some ideas:

- Save your work. Don't just save after you finish a document, save while you are working. The power is sure to go off just as you are on the last line, and if you haven't saved, well...

- If you are experimenting with a document, work on a copy of that document rather than an original. You can make changes freely. If you change your mind, it is easier to go back to the original than to undo any or all changes you may make.

- Make backups. *Backups* are an extra copy of your work (on a floppy disk) that you can fall back on, if necessary. Develop a backup routine and stick to it. See *Using MS-DOS 5* for help with setting up a routine.

Taking Care of the Computer

Take care of the hardware (everything you can see and touch) the same way you would care for your TV or VCR. Don't feed it, water it, drop it, or expose it to extreme heat or cold. Don't plug anything into the computer when it is on.

Take care of the software the same way you would care for audio or video cassettes. Don't leave them out in the heat, don't spill anything on them, don't open the metal shutter, and keep them away from magnets. Keep in mind that all electrical equipment puts out a magnetic field, including the telephone, the electric pencil sharpener, and even the PC itself. This doesn't mean that you have to keep your phone in a desk drawer—just don't keep your disks near the phone. Don't take a disk out of the drive when the light is on.

Always turn off your machine properly. Close all applications, and be sure you are at the DOS prompt. You should not turn off your computer when the screen looks like this:

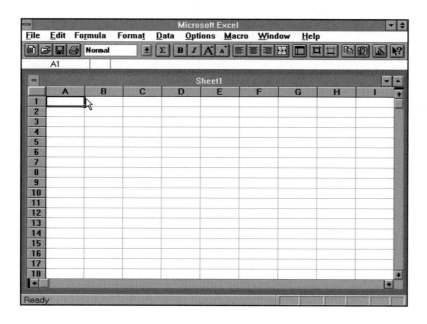

You can turn off your computer when the screen looks like this:

DOs and DON'Ts

As you get more comfortable using your PC, keep the following guidelines in mind:

- Do save your work periodically.
- Do use descriptive file names.
- Do use directories to organize your files.
- Do back up your files.
- Do turn off the computer ONLY at the DOS prompt.
- Do write down any error messages that the computer sends you.
- Do label your disks.
- Do be sure that your computer can run software before you buy the software.
- If you are considering purchasing a computer or software, do ask friends and colleagues what they recommend.
- Do use a surge protector.
- When you purchase new software, do return the registration card. This will ensure that you receive information about the latest versions of the software.

As you begin using your PC, try to avoid the following:

- Don't plug anything into the computer when it is turned on.
- Don't open the system unit when the computer is turned on.
- Don't take a disk out of the drive when the drive light is on.
- Don't turn off the computer while an application is still open.
- Don't force a floppy disk into the disk drive.

- Don't leave disks in an area that is excessively hot.

- Don't spill anything on a floppy disk.

- Don't open the metal shutter of a floppy disk.

- Don't use the original software disks to install or run a program; make copies of the disks and use the copies.

- Don't install someone else's software on your computer; copying software is illegal. You must buy your own copy of the software.

Questions and Answers

What is DOS?

DOS is an acronym for *disk operating system*. DOS manages the details of your system—storing and retrieving programs and files.

Do I need DOS?

You always need DOS—even if you use Microsoft Windows or a DOS shell program (a replacement program).

Where do I get DOS?

When you purchased your computer, you should have received DOS as part of the package. If you didn't, see your dealer. If you want to upgrade (use a newer version of DOS), see your dealer.

What is the difference between MS-DOS and PC DOS?

Different companies license DOS and may name DOS differently. DOS is DOS. As far as you are concerned, there is no difference between these packages.

Do I need a mouse?

Most programs do not require a mouse. Generally, you can perform tasks with the mouse or the keyboard. But some actions may be easier to perform with a mouse. For instance, most Microsoft Windows programs are easier to use if you have a mouse. Also, some tasks—for instance, drawing—require a mouse.

What is an IBM-compatible computer?

IBM manufactures a complete line of personal computers. Other companies make personal computers as well; these computers, called *compatibles* or *clones*, use the same parts as an IBM, use DOS to manage the system, and run the same software as an IBM computer. Often, however, IBM-compatibles cost less than actual IBM computers.

What is the difference between an IBM (or compatible) and the Macintosh?

You use an IBM or compatible and a Macintosh to accomplish the same tasks; both are computers. They differ in the way they operate. A Macintosh computer uses a different operating system—not DOS. Also, a Macintosh computer cannot run software designed for an IBM or compatible. You must purchase software specifically for the Macintosh.

What is RAM?

RAM is short for *random-access memory*. RAM is the temporary storage area of the PC. To keep the information in RAM, you must save it to disk.

What is the difference between RAM and disk space?

Many users confuse RAM and disk space, perhaps because RAM and disk space are measured in the same way. Users say they have 20 megabytes of RAM, but what they mean is they have 20 megabytes of hard disk space. Keep in mind that disk space is permanent storage and RAM is temporary storage. You have more disk space than you do RAM.

What is a backup and why should I back up files?

A backup is an extra copy of your data. In case something happens to the original data, you should always have an up-to-date copy (or *backup*) of the information. When something does go wrong, you can use the backup copy. Be sure that you back up data to a floppy disk—not a different section of the hard disk—and that you store the backup in a safe place—preferably away from the computer so that it will not get mixed up with other disks.

What is a port?

A port is a plug in the back of your system unit. You can plug other equipment (sometimes called *peripherals*) into the computer through these ports. For instance, you connect your printer to the system unit with a cable and a port.

What is an upgrade and why should I upgrade?

An *upgrade* is a change in a software package. The manufacturers may have added new features, fixed problems, and enhanced other features. If these features are crucial to your work, you should consider upgrading. If they are not, you may not want to upgrade.

What is a bug?

A *bug* is a problem with the software—for instance, a feature that does not work as it is supposed to. Software manufacturers usually correct bugs when they upgrade the software.

If I want to purchase a computer, how do I determine the best type of computer for me?

There is no simple answer to this question. The type of computer that is best for you depends on how you plan to use it. If you only plan to use it to keep track of finances and type simple documents, you will not need an expensive computer with a great deal of memory. Purchasing a computer requires some thinking, planning, and research. For information on purchasing a computer, see *Que's Computer Buyer's Guide,* 1992 Edition.

What is a network?

A *network* is several computers connected to each other. Usually one main computer serves as the hub or center of the network. This computer is called the *server* and may store data or programs that all users on the network can access from their computers.

What is a modem?

A *modem* is a peripheral (extra equipment) that you can add to your computer. A modem allows you to communicate through the phone lines to other computers. These computers can be in another building, another state, or even another country.

If I still have questions, where can I get more help?

Que publishes computer books on a wide range of hardware and software topics. These books may further expand your knowledge of the PC. Also, many magazines are devoted to the topic of PCs. These magazines contain current reviews of software programs as well as cover the latest in hardware. Some popular magazines are *InfoWorld*, *PC World*, and *PC Magazine*.

Glossary

3 1/2-inch disk A floppy disk enclosed in a hard plastic case. These disks come in two capacities: 720K and 1.44M.

5 1/4-inch disk A floppy disk enclosed in a flexible plastic case. These disks come in two capacities: 360K and 1.2M.

application A computer program used for a particular task—such as word processing. In most cases, the terms *program* and *software* and *application* mean the same thing and can be used interchangeably.

AUTOEXEC.BAT A file that DOS executes when you start the computer. This file may include commands that control different settings. For example, you may include a command that tells DOS where your programs are located.

backup A copy of data or programs that you make in case the original data or program becomes damaged.

batch file A file that contains a series of DOS commands. The commands are executed when you run the batch file. You may create a batch file that changes to a certain directory and starts a program.

boot The process of loading the operating system.

byte A measure of the amount of information on a disk. A byte is equal to about one character.

capacity A term used to describe how much data you can store on a disk. Capacity is measured in kilobytes (K) or megabytes (M).

central processing unit (CPU) The main chip or "brain" of the computer. The CPU is stored inside the system unit and controls the computer. The speed of your computer partially depends on the CPU. CPUs used in computers are numbered 8088, 8086, 80286, 80386, and 80486. The higher the number, the faster the CPU.

COMMAND.COM An essential DOS file that contains the command processor.

CONFIG.SYS A special file that sets configuration settings. DOS consults this file when it is started. Some applications require special commands. These commands are contained in the CONFIG.SYS file.

click To press and release the mouse button.

Clipboard A temporary spot in memory that holds text or graphics that you cut or copy.

CPU The central processing unit. See *central processing unit*.

cursor A marker used to indicate the current position on-screen.

database An application used to store and retrieve related sets of information—for instance, an inventory list.

density A term used to describe the amount of information you can store on a floppy disk. Double-density disks store 360K or 720K of data; high-density disks store 1.2M or 1.44M of data.

desktop publishing program An application used to create professional-quality documents. These programs combine text formatting and graphics capabilities.

dialog box An on-screen window that displays additional command options. Many times a dialog box reminds you of the consequences or results of a command and asks you to confirm that you want to go ahead with the action.

directory An index to the files stored on disk or a list of files. A directory is similar to a file cabinet; you can group files together in directories.

DOS An acronym for *disk operating system*. DOS manages the details of your system—storing and retrieving programs and files.

DOS prompt The indicator you see on-screen that tells you DOS is ready for a command (for instance, C:>).

double-click Pressing the mouse button twice in rapid succession.

drag Pointing to an item and then pressing and holding down the left mouse button as you move the mouse.

draw program An application program used to create computer graphics—such as a logo.

file The various individual reports, memos, databases, and letters that you store on your hard drive (or disk) for future use.

file name The name that you assign a file when you store it to disk. A file name consists of two parts: the root and the extension. The root can be up to eight characters long. The extension, which is optional, can be three characters long and usually indicates the file type. The root and extension are separated by a period. SALES.DOC is a valid file name; SALES is the root, and DOC is the extension.

file spec The combination of file name and extension, usually with the use of wild cards. The file spec *.DOC means all files with the DOC extension. The file spec MEMO.* means all files named MEMO with any extension.

floppy disk A storage device. Floppy disks come in two sizes (3 1/2-inch and 5 1/4-inch), two densities (double-density and high-density), and different capacities. (5 1/4-inch disks can store either 360K or 1.2M. 3 1/2-inch disks can store either 720K or 1.44M.)

floppy disk drive A device that reads (retrieves) and writes (stores) information on a floppy disk.

format The process that prepares a disk for use.

function keys The keys labeled F1, F2, F3, and so on. The location of the function keys varies, depending on the type of keyboard you have. Different programs use each key differently.

gigabyte One billion bytes. Abbreviated G or Gig.

graphical user interface (GUI) A visual environment that allows a user to learn a computer program more intuitively and to use a computer program more easily. Microsoft Windows is an example of a graphical user interface.

group In Microsoft Windows, a collection of programs. These programs are stored in a group window, which is represented by a group icon.

GUI An abbreviation for *graphical user interface*. The word is pronounced "gooey."

hard disk A data storage device. Hard disks vary in size; they can range from 20M to over 155M. They also vary in type. Some hard disks are encased in the system unit, and you also can have an external hard disk.

hardware The physical parts of the computer: the screen, the keyboard, the mouse, and so on.

icon A picture that represents a group window, an application, a document, or other elements within Microsoft Windows and Microsoft Windows programs.

keyboard An input device. You issue commands to the computer by typing on the keyboard.

kilobyte About one thousand (1024 to be exact) bytes. Kilobytes are used to measure disk capacity and memory.

megabyte One million bytes of information.

memory The part of the computer that stores information.

menu An on-screen list of commands or options.

monitor The piece of hardware—much like a television screen—that displays on-screen what you type on the keyboard.

mouse A pointing device used in some programs to move the mouse pointer on-screen, to select windows, and to issue commands.

mouse pointer The on-screen symbol that moves when you move the mouse. The pointer changes shape depending on the task you are performing (typing text, selecting a command, and so on).

path The route, through directories, to a program or document file. The path C:\REPORTS\SALES\EASTDIV.DOC, for example, includes five elements: the disk drive (C:); the root directory (\); the directory (REPORTS); the subdirectory, which is a directory within the first directory (SALES); and the file name (EASTDIV.DOC).

peripheral Any extra equipment you attach to the computer. For instance, a printer is considered a peripheral.

port The plug in the back of the system unit that you use to connect peripherals. For instance, you can use a port to connect a printer to your system.

program A set of instructions that tells the computer what to do. *Program* means the same thing as *application* or *software*.

RAM An acronym for *random-access memory*. RAM is a temporary place where the computer stores data and program instructions.

resolution A measurement of the quality or the sharpness of your monitor.

root directory The main directory. All other directories are contained in the root directory.

shell A program that acts as a user interface to the features of an operating system.

software Another term for computer programs or applications. You run software on your hardware.

spreadsheet An application that enables you to manipulate numbers. Spreadsheets let you figure complex calculations and do intensive number crunching that would be difficult to do manually.

subdirectory An index to the files stored on disk or a list of files. A directory is similar to a file cabinet; you can group files together in directories. *Subdirectory* means the same thing as *directory*.

syntax The format and rules you follow when issuing a DOS command.

wild card A character used to represent other characters. A question mark (?) wild card matches any single character. An asterisk (*) wild card matches any group of characters.

window In Microsoft Windows and Microsoft Windows programs, a rectangular area on-screen in which you view an application or a document. A window can contain icons that represent applications, the application itself, or a document you have created in an application.

Everything in Microsoft Windows is contained in a window.

word processor An application you can use to manipulate text—type letters, memos, brochures, and so on.

Index

graphical user interface (GUI), 31, 219
graphics, 195-197
group icons, 106-107
group windows, 106-107
groups, files, renaming, 85
GUI (graphical user interface), 31, 219

H

hard disks, 219
    defragmenting utilities, 202
    drives, 14-15, 20
    fine tuning utilities, 202
hardware, 5, 219
    drives, 14-15
    keyboard, 14-15, 20-21
    monitor, 14-15, 20, 220
    mouse, 15, 23-24
    ports, 213
    printers, 16
    system unit, 14-15
help
    additional information, 10
    exiting, 132
    Microsoft Windows, 104-105
    spreadsheet programs, 164-165
    window, closing, 164
    word processing programs, 132-133

I

IBM-compatible computers, 212-213
icons, 31-33, 106-107, 219
inserting
    disks, floppy, 48-49, 54-55
    lines, blank, 135, 138-139
    text, 136-137
insertion point, 24
integrated programs, 198-199
Invalid directory message, 74, 75

J-K

keyboards, 14-15, 20-21, 220
kilobytes (K), 17, 216, 220

L

layout (desktop publishing), 197-198
lines (blank)
    deleting, 138
    inserting, 135, 138-139
listing of tasks, 38-39

M

Macintosh, 213
maintenance, computer, 208-211
marquees, 170
maximizing windows, 112-113
megabytes (M/meg), 17, 20, 216, 220
megahertz (MHz), 16
memory, 220
menu bar, 34, 94
menus, 220
    closing without selecting command, 100
    commands, selecting, 100-101
MHz (megahertz), 16
Microsoft Windows, 31, 188-189
    commands, selecting, 100-101
    Control menu, 33
    desktop, 33
        accessories, 32
        rearranging, 99
    exiting, 102-103
    file management, 32
    help, 104-105
    menu bar, 34
    Program Manager, 98-101
    programs
        exiting, 124-125
        restarting, 103, 125
        starting, 32, 98-99, 122-123
    restarting, 103

N-O

P

Easy PCs